"IF YOUR GOAL IS THE COMM...
THIS CAN BE A PLACE TO PU...

Good nonfiction writing must be like a flawless set of directions, taking readers exactly where the writer wants them to go while making absolutely sure that at no point are they in the slightest danger of losing their way.

This, Barry Tarshis feels, is the fundamental principle that marks the difference between the work of the professional writer and the amateur. Having established this point, he goes on to demonstrate exactly how actual writers succeed—and fail—in producing first-rate material. His selections come from the most famous writers of our time as well as from lesser-known but fully polished pros; from gifted students as well as from well-meaning but awkward amateurs; from nonfiction books, magazines, newspapers, class assignments, and even technical journals. They exemplify virtually every challenge that faces a writer and every technique a writer can make use of—techniques that are more than simply "tricks of the trade," that represent the very essence of writing effectiveness and are the hallmark of the true professional.

HOW TO WRITE LIKE A PRO

BARRY TARSHIS has been a professional free-lance writer since 1964, and during this period has written books, magazine articles, speeches, and advertising copy. He has written, co-authored or ghostwritten fifteen books, and his magazine credits include *Playboy, New York, Harper's Bazaar*, and *Seventeen*. He is a contributing editor to *Tennis Magazine* and a professor in the Graduate School of Communications at Fairfield University.

HOW TO WRITE LIKE A PRO

A Guide to Effective Nonfiction Writing

by Barry Tarshis

WITH A FOREWORD BY
Don McKinney,
Managing Editor, *McCall's* Magazine

A PLUME BOOK
NEW AMERICAN LIBRARY
TIMES MIRROR
NEW YORK AND SCARBOROUGH, ONTARIO

ACKNOWLEDGMENTS

Alfred A. Knopf, Inc. for permission to reprint excerpts from *Crazy
Salad*, by Nora Ephron. Copyright © 1972, 1973, 1974, 1975 by Nora
Ephron.

The New York Times Company for permission to reprint excerpt
from "A Visit with Eudora Welty," by Anne Tyler. Copyright © 1980.

Excerpts from *Quintana and Friends* by John Gregory Dunne. Copyright © 1961, 1965, 1966, 1967, 1969, 1970, 1971, 1973, 1974, 1976, 1977,
1978 by John Gregory Dunne. Reprinted by permission of the pub-
lisher, E. P. Dutton.

PLUME TRADEMARK REG. U.S. PAT. OFF. AND FOREIGN COUNTRIES
REGISTERED TRADEMARK—MARCA REGISTRADA
HECHO EN WESTFORD, MASS., U.S.A.

SIGNET, SIGNET CLASSICS, MENTOR, PLUME, MERIDIAN
and NAL BOOKS are published *in the United States* by The New
American Library, Inc., 1633 Broadway, New York, New York 10019,
in Canada by The New American Library of Canada Limited,
81 Mack Avenue, Scarborough, Ontario M1L 1M8

Library of Congress Cataloging in Publication Data

Tarshis, Barry.
How to write like a pro.

Bibliography: p.
1. Readability (Literary style)
2. Rhetoric. I. Title.
PN204.T37   808'.025   81-22477
ISBN 0-452-25411-6   AACR-2

First Plume Printing, April, 1983

1 2 3 4 5 6 7 8 9

PRINTED IN THE UNITED STATES OF AMERICA

Contents

Acknowledgments

IN certain respects, nearly everyone who has figured one way or another in my writing career helped me write this book, but there are a few people to whom I owe special debts of gratitude. I'm grateful, first of all, to Ted Cheney, at whose invitation I began teaching the writing course I now teach at the Fairfield University Graduate School of Corporate and Political Communication, and to Nick Bakalar, whose patience and judicious editing made this book much better than it might have been with a less demanding editor. I'm grateful, too, to my friend, David Wiltse, who served as a sounding board throughout the project and who offered some valuable suggestions at a couple of crucial points along the way, and to Shep Campbell, who has been helpful for many of my projects. And, as always, I'm grateful to my wife, Karen, my daughter, Lauren, and my son, Andrew, all of whom show me support in more ways than even *they* are aware. I'm grateful, finally, to all of the students I've had in my classes since I began teaching at Fairfield. I first began learning things about writing from my students on the first day I taught, and the learning process continues to this day.

Foreword

by Don McKinney,
Managing Editor, *McCall's* Magazine

MANY years ago I took a writing course from a venerable professor at the University of North Carolina named Phillips Russell, and during the semester he repeated, many times, one of the most useful pieces of writing advice I've ever heard: "Bring on the bear!" For those of you who may not find this of instant value, let me explain. Russell was talking about an article submitted by one of his students which described a bear hunt in the mountains of North Carolina. The student had gone on for page after page telling about the participants in the hunt, the terrain through which they were traveling, the weapons they had taken along, the breakfast they had prepared over a campfire, when Dr. Russell issued his famous command.

This does not mean, of course, that the bear has to lumber out of the woods and fix his beady eyes on the reader on page one; it does mean that you had better let the reader know that bear is coming, and there will be hell to pay when it gets there. And while there is great value in setting a scene and letting the suspense build, you can never let the reader forget for a minute that you have more on your mind than the piney woods and the call of the birds. *You* may know that big things are coming, but if you haven't primed your reader for them, he may be gone before the bear ever gets there.

There are many techniques that allow a writer to do this —from the action lead that then stops in mid-crisis and flashes back, to a simple, low, ominous series of mentions that build a feeling of tension—and they can all be learned. That's what a technique is: the definition is "technical skill" and such skills can be taught, just as can computer programming or fly fishing. I have spent too many years working with writers and editing their articles to ever believe that the ability to write is some inborn skill that you either have or will never get.

I realize, of course, as does Mr. Tarshis, that brilliant writers are not created by writing teachers or even books as good as this one. I remember meeting a young writer from the *National Review* back in the mid-60s; her name was Joan Didion, and not many people had heard of her at the time, but when I saw her writing samples I realized that she was a rare find. I was working on the *Saturday Evening Post* then, and we promptly gave her an assignment and kept her working steadily for us until we went out of business in 1969. Joan didn't need any editing then, and she never did need any; she was, and is, a born writer.

Of course, no amount of technical knowledge instruction will turn an ordinary writer into a Joan Didion or a John McPhee or a Tom Wolfe or a handful of others I could name. But ordinary writers can be taught the tools that professionals use. You can learn how to describe a person or a place so as to bring it alive on the page, how to construct an article so that it has the maximum impact, how to use dialogue intelligently, how to avoid writing articles that sound as if they came out of a computer.

I have never taught a formal course in magazine article writing, but over the past twenty-seven years I have edited thousands of manuscripts, and held endless conversations with writers on just where they went wrong and what they could do to solve the problems. There is nothing really unique about writing as a skill; anybody with a good eye, a curious mind, a reasonable supply of common sense, and a working knowledge of the language can do it. I think this book will help. But don't forget the bear.

1

The Art
of Readability

SOMEONE once said in praise of actor Richard Burton that Burton could recite the telephone book and make it sound interesting. I've often thought the same thing, albeit in a different context, about certain writers. Certain writers—and I'm talking here about writers of nonfiction, not novelists or poets—can capture and sustain your interest no matter what they're writing about. Their writing has an ease and a smoothness to it, and even when the subject is complicated you rarely find yourself struggling to figure out what these writers are saying because they somehow always manage to make what they write about accessible, interesting, and engaging. There is something uniquely compelling about the way these writers present their material: you feel when reading them that they are not so much writing as *talking* directly to you; and you like the voice you hear. They strike you, these writers, as people you'd like to get to know better, if only to shoot the breeze with every now and then.

Not surprisingly, the writers I have in mind are at the top of their profession, and you've probably read their articles, essays, and, in some cases, books. Among the many writers I place in this category are John McPhee, Tom Wolfe, E. B. White, Gay Talese, Nora Ephron, Gary Wills, Lewis Thomas, John Gregory Dunne, Joan Didion, and Anatole Broyard. Although they write about different subjects and have different styles, these writers—as well as the many other contemporary writers whose work we'll be looking at throughout this book—all share one common quality: they are all highly *readable*. You enjoy reading them not only because of *what* they say but because of *how* they say it. And the main purpose of this book is to examine just what it is about these writers that makes them so readable, and what you, as an aspiring writer, can learn from them.

This book is based on a simple but by no means obvious premise. The premise is that readability—that is to say, how smoothly, clearly, and engagingly a piece of writing *reads*—can be understood within the context of certain specific writing techniques—techniques, however, that are only tangentially related to the so-called mechanics of writing and are rarely mentioned in the typical "how-to" writing book. The techniques I'm referring to here relate to the overall *presentation* of your material: how you organize it, shape it, and control the flow of it. They relate to the tone you strike and sustain throughout a piece, the sense of authority, wit, and humanity you build into it. Above all, these techniques relate to how successfully you tailor your material to the unique but often dimly understood demands of the *reading* experience.

Allow me to clarify this premise—to explain how the approach I am taking in this book differs from what seems to me to be the conventional approach to writing instruction. In general, writing courses and "how-to" books on writing are pretty much word- or mechanics-oriented. The notion seems to be that you become a better writer by learning how to use words more precisely, more succinctly, and more imaginatively. You become, in short, a more efficient word mechanic.

I don't discount the importance of basic stylistic mechanics in writing, and I'm not one of those persons who argue that a writer has more important things to worry about than spelling, punctuation, and the basics of sentence construction. But once we enter the realm of highly *readable* nonfiction writing, we begin to encounter technical elements that can't be explained—at least not adequately—within the framework of the basic principles of composition. Ultimately, the technical elements I'm referring to here have to do with your ability as a writer *to control the experience your reader goes through as he reads what you've written*—to control not only the manner in which the reader processes and digests your information but the way he reacts to it as well. More than anything else, in my judgment, it is this ability—the degree to which you, as a writer, assume and exercise control over your reader—that determines how readable your writing is; and more than anything else, it is this degree of control that separates accomplished writers from mediocre writers.

Beyond "Talent"

That there are specific techniques, apart from what we normally think of as the basic mechanics of writing, which can enhance readability is something I myself was not really aware of until about four years ago, even though I have been earning my living as a freelance writer since the mid-1960s. Indeed, if you had asked me four years ago to explain the difference between nonfiction writers who were engaging and compelling to read and writers who weren't, I would have said, "talent." If you had pressed further, I would have mentioned "imagination," "inspiration," "creativity," and "sensibility." If you had suggested to me four years ago that I would someday be writing a book built around the techniques of readability, I would have said you were crazy.

Don't misunderstand. I have long contended that anybody of average intelligence can learn to write in a reasonably clear, straightforward fashion. But to write with any noticeable degree of élan, polish, or professionalism—well, that was quite another matter. For this you needed "talent." Like superior hand and eye coordination, or a perfect ear for music, keeping a reader engaged was a facility you had to be born with. You couldn't learn it from a book.

I considered myself living evidence of this "truth." Writing was always my best subject in school, and as far back as I can remember teachers were telling me that I had a "flair" for writing, and a "way with words." Consequently, I never gave much thought to the actual process through which I was able to involve my readers with the thoughts and the images that filled my articles and books. I would sit down at my typewriter, think of what I wanted to say, and start to type. Every two or three paragraphs I'd look to see if what I'd written looked and sounded okay. If it didn't, I'd change things around: shift the order of phrases, substitute words, maybe ditch a paragraph or two, and start again. I always had a vague idea of what I wanted to say, but I had no way of predicting when I fed a fresh piece of paper into my typewriter how far down the page I would get before I yanked the paper out, scrunched it up, and tossed it into the wastebasket. In retrospect, I worked at my craft like some photographers I know who shoot dozens of rolls on each job, figuring the law of averages will assure them at least one or two acceptable shots. "Flair" or "way with words" notwithstanding, I would not have lasted a year as a freelancer had I not had the will (and the sturdy back) to stay planted at the typewriter until something I wrote took on a sound and a shape that met what I considered professional standards. Even then, it wasn't until an editor called to tell me that he or she liked what I'd handed in that I was able to relax in the knowledge that I'd done a creditable job.

All of which is another way of saying that I had no business accepting an offer I received in the spring of 1977 from Theodore Cheney, a writer and teacher who was heading the professional writing program at Fairfield University's Graduate School of Corporate and Political Communication. Cheney obviously assumed that because I had been earning my living as a professional writer for the previous thirteen years, I was qualified to teach a nonfiction writing course that would address itself to the qualities which separate "professional" writers from "aspiring" writers, and I was too vain to give him reason for assuming otherwise. In Cheney's defense, he didn't make the offer until he'd observed me working with students in one of his seminars, but I suspect he mistook my enthusiasm—I genuinely enjoyed working with the students—for expertise. In any event, during the summer of 1977, I found myself getting ready to teach college students how to do something I wasn't sure how I did myself.

Well, Cheney's invitation produced an interesting result: it forced me to take a hard, analytical look at what I had been up to for the previous thirteen years when I was writing my best pieces, and at what writers I admire are up to when they turn out pieces that I find particularly engaging and readable. The more I read and reread pieces and passages from pieces by nonfiction writers whose craft I have always held in high esteem, the more I began to see certain effects I had once attributed to "talent" could, in fact, be understood in terms of technique.

I noticed, for instance, that whenever they were explaining something complicated, good writers didn't simply dump a lot of information in your lap and leave it up to you to sort it all out and make sense of it. They fed you the information in easily digestible portions. Certain sentences, in fact, served no other function than to put you in a more receptive frame of mind for the *next* piece of information. In other words, the writers weren't merely presenting information, they were "staging" it for you, making it easy for you to figure out the relative importance of the various ideas and details that made up the presentation.

I noticed, too, that keeping pace with these writers was never much of a problem because they were always directing your focus, sometimes with a word, sometimes with a sentence. What's more, these writers had an uncanny way of sensing when you might be slipping away from their grasp, might be getting a little bored or itchy or confused. You could point to certain sentences that served no other apparent function than to reinforce the writer's grip on the reader—in effect, to *reclaim* the reader.

I couldn't help but notice, too, that these writers managed to convey in their work a quality I can only describe as "immediacy." They managed to make me feel close to whatever they happened to be writing about. They gave me the feeling that they weren't so much writing *for* me as sharing *with* me what they wanted to say. Let me cite just a few passages to show you what I mean.

From Michael Herr's *Dispatches:*

There were times during the night when all the jungle sounds would stop at once. There was no dwindling down or fading away, it was all gone in a single instant as though some signal had been transmitted out to the life: bats, birds, snakes, monkeys, insects, picking up on a frequency that a thousand years in the jungle might condition you to receive, but leaving you as it was to wonder what you weren't hearing now, straining for any sound, one piece of information. I had heard it before in other jungles, the Amazon and the Philippines, but those jungles were "secure," there wasn't much chance that hundreds of Viet Cong were coming and going, moving and waiting, living out there just to do you harm. The thought of that one could turn any sudden silence into a space that you'd fill with everything you thought was quiet in you, it could even put you on the approach to clairaudience. You thought you heard impossible things; damp roots breathing, fruit sweating, fervid bug action, the heartbeat of tiny animals.

From John Gregory Dunne, in the introduction to his book of essays, *Quintana and Friends:*

> I think I became a writer because I stuttered. I still stutter, although I can disguise it so well that unless I am tired or drunk the stammer is almost imperceptible. Like all stutterers, I have my own Distant Early Warning system. I have become adept at recognizing two or three sentences ahead of time those hard consonants that will trip me up and I have a warehouse of soft and sibilant synonyms to transport me across the shoals of speech. The effect of this personal DEW line is to give my diction an odd, herky-jerky cadence, making me sound like nothing so much as a simultaneous translation into English from another language.

From a John Leonard book review in the *New York Times* of Harold T. P. Hayes's *Three Levels of Time:*

> The Sahara is important. It gobbles up three million acres a year to improve its desert. Only the acacia tree fights back. While the acacia waits around for a rainfall that occurs once every 10 years, everybody eats it: little creatures go at the roots, the medium-size gnaw on the bark and the big guys munch on the sun-drenched leaves.
>
> An acacia is rather like a reviewer, waiting to be leaked upon by genius and being nibbled at by rabbits, gazelles and giraffes. We have overgrazed the Sahara; we have probably overgrazed the earth, eating up its mineral veins. As for our grandchildren, let them eat sand.

From Joan Didion's profile of Joan Baez in *Slouching Towards Bethlehem:*

> She lives quietly. She reads, and she talks to the people who have been told where she lives, and occasionally she

and Ira Sandperl go to San Francisco to see friends, to talk about the peace movement. She sees her two sisters and she sees Ira Sandperl. She believes that her days at the Institute talking and listening to Ira Sandperl are bringing her closer to contentment than anything she has done so far. "Certainly more than singing. I used to stand up there and think I'm getting so many thousand dollars, and for what?" She is defensive about her income ("Oh, I have some money from somewhere"), vague about her plans. "There are some things I want to do. I want to try some rock 'n' roll and some classical music. But I'm not going to start worrying about the charts and the sales because then where are you?"

Most people would agree, I think, that each of these paragraphs is nicely turned out, that each *reads* exceptionally well. But why? Why are these paragraphs so readable, so cohesive, so immediate? Part of the reason, undoubtedly, is the intelligence, the observant eye, the sensibility, and the wit that each of these writers brings to the material; and part of it has to do with words they choose and the way they mount their sentences.

But look for a moment at Herr's paragraph. Notice how much he relies on the pronoun "you," even though his book is written in the first person.

Look at Dunne's paragraph. Notice how the word "stutterer" is repeated in each of the first three sentences. Notice how either the word itself or some allusion to it is threaded throughout the paragraph. Notice how Dunne supplies the phrase "personal DEW line" in the last sentence even though we don't really *need* these three words to tell us that "this" refers to the Distant Early Warning system mentioned earlier.

Now look at the John Leonard paragraph again. Why did Leonard make "The Sahara is important" a separate sentence instead of writing, as someone else might have done,

"The importance of the Sahara is that it gobbles up three million acres a year to improve its desert"? And why did he place "Only the acacia tree fights back" before the sentence describing all the nasty things that happen to the acacia while it waits around for a rainfall? And what about the phrase "big guys"? Isn't that phrase a little out of place in a *New York Times* book review?

Read the Joan Didion paragraph again. There is quoted material here, but why did Ms. Didion choose to present it in this precise manner? Why did she put some of the quoted material in parentheses, and why did she break up the two main quotes with the statement, "She is defensive about her income"?

I won't attempt to answer any of these questions specifically at this point, for we will be examining at length throughout the rest of this book the technical concepts embodied in these passages. Rest assured, though, that in each of these situations there is not only talent at work but an identifiable *technique* as well—a technique whose ultimate effect is to enhance the readability of the paragraph.

Which raises an intriguing question: were these writers *consciously* using these techniques as they were writing these paragraphs? I wish I knew, but I don't. I suspect not. My suspicion is that each of these writers *intuitively* uses the techniques I'm talking about. Each writer probably has an innate "feel" or an "ear" for what works best in getting across to the reader with clarity and impact a thought or a feeling. Each writer has a built-in sense of how to keep his or her readers engaged and involved. As Frank Deford, a *Sports Illustrated* staff writer who writes as readably as anyone I know, once told me, "I'm not really aware of any specific techniques I use to keep my readers involved. I'm just concerned at all times about losing a reader's interest, and I want to keep him on the hook."

Not that it matters. For whether or not a writer is consciously aware of a technique that is enhancing the readability of his material, the technique is nonetheless there, and identifiable; and as such it can be understood and quantified and, more important, adopted by other writers. And here, in short, is the premise on which I built the course I teach at Fairfield University and around which I've written this book. My contention is that a good deal of what makes the best nonfiction writers of our time so readable are techniques that have been either ignored or given short shrift by writing teachers and authors of writing books. I maintain, moreover, that any writer who puts his mind to it can incorporate these techniques into his own writing style and, in the process, improve the readability of his own writing.

Mind you, I'm not saying that the top writers are not blessed with a measure of talent lacking in less accomplished writers. For just as there are people who seem to be born with attributes that make them ideally suited to a particular sport, so are there people who seem to have been programmed from conception to be good writers. But what I'm going to try to do in this book—and what I try to do each week in my class—is to demystify the "talent" aspect of writing: not to dismiss its significance, surely, but to show that much of what we admire and respond to in the top nonfiction writers today needn't be attributed entirely to that ineffable quality known as talent, but can be quantified, studied, and learned.

What This Book Can—and Can't— Teach You

When a friend of mine who is a successful writer heard I was working on a book about writing, he suggested, with all due respect, that I was wasting my time. People with talent, and the urge to write, he said, learn to write on their own—by doing it. People who lack the talent and the urge, he said, aren't going to learn to write with any measure of professionalism no matter what you put in a book.

My friend, of course, is right—to an extent. Like any skill or art form, writing embodies a dimension that for all intents and purposes is indeed unteachable. You can't really *teach* imagination, or insight, or wit, or sensitivity, or that elusive quality of mind usually referred to as sensibility. (As Norman Mailer once said of James Jones: Jones was the "only one of us who had the beer guts of a broken-glass brawl"—this you don't teach.) Neither can you teach (within the framework of a writing course, at any rate) the self-discipline, the persistence, and the tolerance for pain and frustration you need if you're serious about being a good enough writer to make a living at it. Writing is frequently characterized as one of the more glamorous ways of earning a dollar, yet I've never met a successful writer who didn't find it an arduous and often painful process. "The most enjoyable part of my typical writing day," John McPhee once said, "is driving my daughters to nursery school."

And even if it's true, as I maintain, that readability is far more teachable than many people think, let's not forget that readability is only one of the many criteria by which a piece of written work or, for that matter, a writer is to be judged. The fact that an essay, an article, or a book is easy and enjoyable to read doesn't necessarily mean that it is accurate or informative, or has any substance; nor is there necessarily a correlation between the readability of a book and its commercial or critical success. Indeed, in most nonfiction writing, *what* you have to say is as important as, if not more important than, *how* you say it. Woodward and Bernstein didn't become best-selling authors because they wrote more readably than other journalists, but because they had the persistence, the energy, the courage, and the resourcefulness to break open the Watergate conspiracy. And although James Joyce is universally acknowledged as one of the greatest writers who ever lived, Joyce's masterpiece, *Ulysses,* is hardly the book anybody would choose as a textbook for a course on readable writing.

All of which is another way of saying that I'm not trying to jam readability down your typewriter. If you write for purely personal reasons and it satisfies a need, or if you don't care how hard your readers have to work or how they respond to what you write, then readability needn't concern you. On the other hand, if your goal as a writer is to publish articles in general-interest publications (as opposed to technical journals, where readability is important but secondary to the material itself) or if you are in a job in which it is important that you *communicate* your ideas, readability assumes more relevance. Whether it pleases you or not, you have little choice but to make your reader an active partner in the writing transaction. And as you will soon see, you're going to have to work harder at the relationship than he is.

I think this book can help you—more, perhaps, than other books on writing you may have read. I don't claim to have discovered any new "secrets" of writing, nor am I offering in this book a "system" or a formula for readable writing. I'm not even saying that you won't find some of the techniques I'll be talking about in this book in other writing books, in slightly different form.

But I do think that my approach to teaching writing is much different from the approaches taken in other writing books I'm familiar with, and I'm pleased to report that I've enjoyed a good deal of success with the students I teach at Fairfield University. No, I haven't turned out any Tom

Wolfes or Joan Didions yet, but you should see the difference between the papers that get handed in at the beginning of each term and those that get handed in at the end. For what it's worth, my students report that they come away from the course with more confidence in their ability to write. And I think, too, that my own ability to write readably has been enhanced by what I've learned through my teaching experience. I won't say that writing is no longer a struggle for me, but I have more control than I used to have over what I do when I write. The proof of it, I guess, is that I'm writing more than ever, but spending a lot less money on typing paper.

Before You Start

As I indicated earlier, this is a *technically* oriented book, but I wouldn't presume to suggest that simply learning how to recognize and use the techniques I talk about in this book will guarantee that you'll be able to incorporate these techniques into your presentation.

Hardly. There is to writing a psychological dimension whose impact influences every phase of the writing process but whose dynamics go far beyond the scope of this book. The confidence you have in your ideas and opinions, the importance you attach to the judgments of other people, the interplay between the critical side of your mind and the noncritical creative side—each of these psychological considerations will go a long way to determine how much effort you have to put into your writing and, ultimately, how vividly and smoothly you're able to express yourself on paper—independent of the techniques you have in your writing arsenal.

Since I'm not a psychiatrist or psychologist, I wouldn't presume to offer you any advice on how to increase the confidence you have in your ideas and opinions, how to diminish the importance you attach to the judgments of other people, or how to bring into more productive balance the interplay between the judgmental and nonjudgmental sides of your mind. But you ought to know, if you don't already, that every writer, even the most accomplished professional—*particularly* the most accomplished professional—has to deal with, and overcome, these problems in his or her own way and on his or her own terms. Writing, by its very nature, is a complex, unwieldy enterprise made up of numerous stages—thinking, organizing, presenting, polishing, etc.—each stage calling for different skills and a different mental approach. What's more, there is a direct correlation, I think, between the ability to write effectively and the capacity to operate, at least for a time, in a kind of twilight zone of chaos and uncertainty. Solidly written, smoothly flowing, and highly readable paragraphs don't just materialize. The thoughts embodied in these paragraphs have to be born, nurtured, shaped and reshaped, and finally cast into sentences that themselves may require any number of revisions before they're ready for reader consumption. Show me a writer worth reading whose first drafts read as smoothly and convincingly as his final drafts, and I'll show you a genius.

I mention all of this not to discourage you but to emphasize a point that can never be emphasized enough about writing. It's hard work: it takes time, it takes effort, it takes a special kind of discipline. Time, effort, and discipline alone, of course, won't make you a good writer—not unless you have the skills to put your time, effort, and discipline to productive use. But skills alone won't make you a good writer, either—not without time, effort, or discipline. This book will teach you techniques that will sharpen your writing skills and help make your writing more readable. But how you put these techniques to use is up to you.

2

Developing Reader Sensitivity

ONE of the things I do routinely in my writing class is to read student papers aloud and then prod the class for comments. I don't usually identify the student whose paper I'm reading, but it frequently doesn't matter. What happens is that most students whose work is getting roughed up by the class almost invariably spring to the defense of what they've written, often with impatience and indignation. They can't understand—or forgive, in many cases—the density of mind that prevents the rest of us in the class from understanding (not to mention appreciating) what they wrote.

I don't mean to be smug. Truth be told, nearly all of us who think of ourselves as writers would do more than our share of squirming if we were privy to the reactions of the people who read our material. It might distress us to discover, for instance, that many of our readers haven't the vaguest idea of what we're talking about even though *we're* convinced that we're being as clear as mountain water. It might surprise us to discover that some of our readers are interpreting literally what we want them to interpret tongue-in-cheek (or, just as bad, interpreting tongue-in-cheek what we want them to interpret literally). And it might be sobering for us to see just how much of what we write is boring or off-putting to our readers.

Yet I can think of few experiences more valuable (and

more humbling) to a writer than to witness firsthand how his readers are responding. For there is probably no better way of developing what may well be the most important attribute you can have as a writer: something I call reader sensitivity.

I define reader sensitivity as an ongoing awareness of how your readers are processing and reacting to what you've written. It's being able to put yourself in your reader's shoes. It's sensing when the word or phrase you've used may not be expressing as clearly as it should the idea or image you're trying to get across. It's sensing when an idea or image you've given your reader is likely to have created a question in the reader's mind (which you must quickly answer). It's sensing when you need to beef up an idea with added details so that your reader will better grasp the importance of the idea. And it's being able to sense when your reader may be getting bored or possibly angry, and knowing what to do to eliminate the boredom or defuse the anger.

In accomplished writers, reader sensitivity appears to be intuitive, in the same way that some entertainers have an innate feel for how an audience is responding to their performance well *before* the curtain and the applause. Certain writers seem to sense *as* they're writing when their material is likely to confuse, overburden, or irritate their readers, and they take immediate measures to counteract these reactions. They don't have to remind themselves to do this. It's all part of the mental set they bring to writing.

But in the event this awareness is *not* an intuitive part of what you, as a writer, bring to writing, you are operating under an all but fatal handicap, and you will remain handicapped until you sensitize yourself to the likely responses of your readers. Indeed most of the problems in the writing that gets churned out daily in schools, businesses, government offices and, more often than you might imagine, in magazines, newspapers, and books can be traced to a writer's failure to take into account *what is going on inside the mind of the person reading his material.* The point I find myself repeating over and over to my students is that too often they seem to be writing in a vacuum; they don't worry enough that their readers might not understand or care about what they've written. I sense too often in student papers an assumption that the writer and the reader are equal partners in the transaction and, as such, should be putting in an equal amount of effort to make the relationship work. If a reader is having trouble understanding what the writer is saying—well, too bad. The reader is simply going to have to work harder.

Would that the writer/reader relationship *were* an equal partnership, with the reader disposed to work as hard at understanding what the writer is trying to say as the writer works to say it. Unfortunately, it isn't. In most writing situations, especially when you're being *paid* to write, you, as a writer, have little choice but to cater to your reader. What's more, you have plenty of competition for the reader's attention. As William Zinsser, in his splendid book, *On Writing Well,* puts it:

> a reader is a person with an attention span of about twenty seconds who is assailed on every side by forces competing for his time, by newspapers and magazines, by television and stereo, by his wife and children and pets, by his house and his yard and all the gadgets he has bought to keep them spruce, and by that most potent of competitors, sleep. The man snoozing in his chair with an unfinished magazine open in his lap is a man who was being given too much unnecessary trouble by the writer.

That's the *good* news. The bad news is that as a writer, you're also competing with the reader himself. For the reader does more than simply *register* the thoughts and images you deliver to him as if he were a check-out person in a supermarket, ringing up and bagging food items. He is constantly working to fit these ideas and images into the fabric of his own mind, constantly relating newly processed ideas and images to his own knowledge and experience. Readers don't simply *read*. They evaluate what you write: agree with it, disagree with it, identify with it, become angry or uncomfortable because of it. And all the while, readers are asking themselves if it's worth their while to read on, or if their time might not be spent more enjoyably reading something else, listening to music, watching television, or just staring into space. In the event the information you're offering is of such cosmic importance that your readers feel as though they *must* read you, you probably don't have to concern yourself terribly much with these reader reactions. Otherwise, the burden of keeping your readers involved is on you. And if enough of your material confuses your readers, makes them work harder than they want to work, or rubs them the wrong way, you're not going to hold on to them for very long. They're tough nuts to crack, your readers, and the worst part is, you need them a lot more than they need you.

But not to worry. Readers, after all, are only human; their affections and attention are up for grabs. And you can win their attention in a number of ways: by offering information that can measurably improve their lives; by getting them hooked on a good story; by making them laugh; by introducing them to people and to subjects they care about. But before you can do any of these things, you have to first understand your readers and you have to sympathize with what they are up against when they're reading. So before going any further, let's take a brief look at who your readers are, and what it takes to make them your allies in the writer/reader transaction.

Getting to Know Your Reader

Step one to becoming a more reader-sensitive writer is to understand reading as a mental process—that is, to understand what the reader has to do to perform his role in the writer/reader transaction. As you might expect, the neuro-physiological dynamics of this process are staggeringly complex, so I won't even attempt to delve into them, but there are three easily understood phases of the process that it behooves you as a writer to become familiar with. I label these as follows: (1) the association phase; (2) the connection phase; and (3) the reaction phase. Let's take a look at each phase, what it entails, and how you can assume a more active role in controlling it.

The Association Phase: From Image to Word to Image

Communication between writer and reader is essentially a matter of producing in the mind of one person—the reader—an idea or image which originates (usually in a nebulous form) in the mind of somebody else: the writer. Some trick! The medium through which you duplicate these ideas and images is, of course, words. But the words serve a different function for each party in the transaction. You use words to express an idea or image *you have already formed* in your mind. Your reader uses words to *form* an idea or image that *doesn't yet exist* in his mind. You know, before you put words to paper, what you want to say and you don't need the words to produce this understanding. The reader, poor soul, has *only* the words on the written page to create the idea or image you want to convey.

The more you ponder this dilemma—the fact that you, as a writer, have a general idea of what you want to say *before* you choose your words, whereas your reader has nothing *but* the words to work with—the more it should underscore in your mind how vital it is that you (1) have a clear idea of what you want to say *before* you write; and (2) choose your words and construct your phrases with precision. The fact that a sentence or a phrase is clear to you is no guarantee that your reader will find it equally clear; and the more familiar you are with the ideas or images you're trying to get across to the reader, the greater the risk that you will inadvertently leave your reader in the dark.

As an example of what I'm talking about, here's the opening paragraph of a piece that appeared not long ago in a regional magazine.

> Personalized license tags or vanity plates, as some refer to them, provide an opportunity for individuals to creatively express themselves while adding that very personal touch to their automobile. For the frustrated writer, it provides a captured audience when being issued a summons or caught in bumper to bumper traffic.

The writer here is telling us about personalized license plates, and we must assume that were he with us, he could easily explain what he is trying to get across in the second sentence. Without this explanation, however, we're in trouble.

Take the phrase "frustrated writer." The writer obviously knows what this phrase is meant to represent. But I find the phrase annoyingly ambiguous. Is the writer referring to himself, or to people in general who are frustrated writers? And why are the writers frustrated—because they can't get published, or because nobody will read what they write?

Look at "captured audience." First of all, the idiom is *captive* audience, not *captured* audience. But either way, it doesn't do the job. It doesn't generate in my mind the image the writer has in his mind—not right away. I have to read the sentence two or three times before I see what the writer meant: motorists stuck in traffic with no choice but to read a personalized license message. I'm not a mind reader, and I don't like to work this hard when I read, particularly when the subject is of no great significance to me.

You may think I'm nitpicking, but I'm doing so for good reason. It's the rare reader who has much tolerance for ambiguous writing, who is willing to reread a sentence two or three times to figure out what the writer is driving at. Yet, more often than not, the first batches of student papers I receive each session suggest a collective notion that all a writer need do is give the reader a rough idea of what he, the writer, is trying to say, and the reader himself will be only too happy (not to mention honored) to fill in the details. Here's a typical example from a student paper which was written as a guide to the bachelor shopper.

> The art of smelling is rapidly declining due to the advent of cellophaned produce, but smelling is still to be found in precincts where supermarkets maintain their ethnic aromas.

The idea the writer wants to get across is that in certain ethnic neighborhoods, where the food is out in the open and not covered in cellophane, supermarkets still smell of food. But "ethnic aromas" is too ambiguous a phrase to communicate this idea. The *writer* understood the image he wanted to convey, but assumed that I would attach to "ethnic aromas" the same association that he attached to it.

Here's yet another example, this from a published piece, that reveals the same *lack* of reader sensitivity.

I had hoped my debut at the Vic Braden Tennis College would be as discreet as the California sun peeping over the hillside. Unfortunately, though, my dazzling white shoes, and equally dazzling white Bostonian skin, put the lie to my air of nonchalance as I strode to the court.

Okay, here we have a narrator explaining how difficult it was to remain inconspicuous on the day she made her debut at the Vic Braden Tennis College, the problem being that her clean shoes and pale complexion made being inconspicuous impossible. But the writing here, although it has a nice professional *sound* to it, is rife with ambiguity—an ambiguity that stems from the writer's failure to recognize that what is clear to her isn't necessarily clear to the reader.

Look at the first sentence again. We can assume that the sight of the sun "peeping over the hillside" conveyed to the writer the idea of discretion. But if you haven't seen what the writer has seen, the phrase "as discreet as the California sun peeping over the hillside" can't help jarring you. You simply don't associate "California sun" with the term "discreet."

In the next sentence, the writer talks about the things —"dazzling white shoes, and equally dazzling white Bostonian skin," (and what is "Bostonian skin" anyway: do Bostonians have different skin from, say, Philadelphians, or New Yorkers?)—that "put the lie to [her] air of nonchalance" as she strode to the court. A nice thought, except that there is a telling difference between trying to be "discreet" and attempting an "air of nonchalance."

I could cite dozens of similar examples from published pieces and from student papers—all illustrating the same failing: the writers not being precise enough in their choice of words to insure that the reader makes the association the writers had in mind. One student paper I received re-

cently talked about the "casual beauty" of the Italian coun-
tryside, as if any reader would know instantly what image
to formulate on the basis of that phrase. Another student,
in a paper having to do with keeping her house free of
insects, explained that in order to keep ants at bay, she had
to "spray their private entrances." The sentence, predict-
ably, drew a big laugh out of the students in the class who
had bawdy minds.

No need to bludgeon the point to death. The message is
simple enough. It isn't up to your reader to convert your
ambiguous phrases into *specific* ideas and images. Nor, for
that matter, is it in the best interest of communication to
allow your reader to do so. Disregard the associations your
words and phrases produce in the mind of your readers, and
you run a constant risk that what you think you are saying
to your reader is not what your reader is hearing. Above
all, effective writing presupposes a oneness between the
idea or image that originates in the mind of the writer and
the idea or image that winds up in the mind of the reader.
It is up to you, the writer, to keep this oneness from split-
ting apart.

The Connection Phase: Making Sure Things Fit

If the only thing you had to worry about when you write
was making sure your reader makes the appropriate associations, writing would be a good deal simpler than it is. No
such luck, for at the same time the reader is converting
your words into ideas and images, he must also connect
each newly processed idea or image to an idea or image he
already has on file in his brain. Should you follow the mention of a restaurant, for instance, with a few phrases about
food, the reader will automatically connect the food phrases
to the idea of a restaurant. Mention a movie and follow it

with the name of an actor or actress, and the reader will connect the actor to the movie. Automatically.

Such is the way the brain of the reader is programmed to operate—not only to convert words into ideas and images but also to figure out where to stick each newly converted idea or image. Whether you're aware as you write or not, and whether you're in control or not, the brain of the reader takes each new idea or image it processes and tries to attach it to an image or idea it already has on file. If everything goes according to plan, the connection will "take," which is to say there will be a logical relationship between the newly processed idea or image and the idea or image already on file. Sometimes, however, the connection doesn't work, in which case the reader's brain has to retrace its steps. It has to disconnect the idea or image it connected milliseconds earlier; it has to put this piece of unconnected information on "hold."

As it happens, the brain is versatile enough to keep a certain amount of "unconnected" information on what we're describing as "hold." But its "holding" capacity is more limited than you might think. The more pieces of unconnected information the brain has to carry at any given time, the longer it takes for the brain to connect *new* ideas and images. Why? Because the presence of unconnected information now obliges the brain to "choose" where it should be connecting the next piece of information it processes.

Imagine a filing cabinet. As long as everything you have to file goes into only one of two different folders, filing is a simple and rapid activity. But each new folder you put inside the file cabinet complicates the job of filing, lengthening the time it takes to decide which piece of paper goes into which folder.

To give you a better idea of what I'm talking about, look at the following sentence:

> Nearly every time I drive from Stamford to Fairfield on the Thruway, I have the same upsetting experience with truckers.

Here we have a piece of straightforward information—a writer telling us something that's easy to understand. But this statement does more than simply *tell* us something. It creates in the mind of the reader the question: *what* upsetting experience? The reader's brain is now looking for an answer to that question. Indeed, it is *expecting* an answer to this question within the next sentence or two. It has what amounts to a "file," marked "same upsetting experience with truckers." If you don't provide this answer you're going to disrupt the delicate process through which the reader must absorb and connect new information at virtually the same time.

So here we have one of the few "rules" of writing I will be setting down in this book: *you must always know what you have led your reader to expect by virtue of the information you've just presented, and you must pay heed to this expectation one way or another*.

Let's take the above example a step further.

> Nearly every time I drive from Stamford to Fairfield on the Thruway, I have the same upsetting experience with truckers. Last week, for example, I was having a cup of coffee at a Howard Johnson's. I was in a great mood. Then, as soon as I got on the road, a trucker started to bear in on my tail, honking his horn.

As written, this paragraph gives the reader little choice but to connect the "upsetting experience" with "having a cup of coffee at a Howard Johnson's." But, as we later see, the coffee has nothing to do with the upsetting experience. We see two sentences later that this connection isn't what the writer had in mind, but in the meantime we're obliged to make a connection we must then turn around and discon-

nect. This business of having to connect and then disconnect ideas is bothersome to all but the most tolerant of
readers. Force the readers to do this often enough, and
you'll find yourself with fewer and fewer of them.

Here's a more obvious example, from a student who was
writing about his experiences in a swimming class.

> Breathing isn't the only concern I've had to overcome.
> There are many good swimmers who wait in the adjacent
> whirlpool. It is the social club.

The phrase "isn't the only concern" leads us to think that
the next piece of information will represent yet *another*
concern. But connecting "There are many good swimmers
who wait in the adjacent whirlpool" with the previous idea
only creates confusion. The problem here is that the writer
hasn't taken that extra step or two to prevent the momen-
tary connecting confusion. Here's a revision that remedies
the problem.

> Breathing isn't the only concern I've had to overcome.
> I've also had to deal with the social aspect of swimming. A
> lot of the better swimmers like to hang out afterward in the
> whirlpool adjacent to the pool, and they treat this gather-
> ing-place like an exclusive social club.

Let's look at one more example that illustrates why the
brain's impulse to connect should figure prominently in
your writing decisions.

> When Susan began going through the mail that morning,
> she noticed a small package wrapped in brown paper. Inside
> the package she could hear something ticking. Susan was
> dressed in a white blouse and blue slacks.

The first sentence here draws our attention to the brown
paper bag. It creates a "file" in our minds. The second sentence tells us immediately, with the phrase "inside the

package," that this new information should be directed to that "file." But what about the third sentence? How does what Susan was wearing connect logically to the ticking package? It doesn't. So what the brain (I think) does in this situation is to create a *new* file. It is now "holding" two pieces of information: one has to do with the package making the ticking sound; the other has to do with Susan's clothes. Now instead of having a *single* focal point to which it can connect new information, the brain has an additional concern. We've blurred its focus. Read on:

> When Susan began going through the mail that morning, she noticed a small package wrapped in brown paper. Inside the package she could hear something ticking. Her face turned as white as the blouse she was wearing.

In this revision, we learn that Susan was wearing a white blouse, but we don't run into the connecting problem. Why? Because we're operating with only one file. Our focus isn't split.

Sometimes, I should point out, a writer—particularly a novelist—will deliberately create a "holding pattern" in the mind of a reader as a means of building suspense. But this is a tricky device and I don't recommend it for most nonfiction writing. The reader's brain has a limited holding capacity. Each time you feed it a piece of information that doesn't logically connect to an idea or image already on file, you force the reader to split his focus and you thereby slow down the reading process. Making clear where you want a reader to connect a particular piece of information involves a technique we'll be discussing in the next chapter. For now, let me emphasize that you must constantly keep in mind the reader's need to find a connecting place (and find it easily) for each new piece of information you're asking him to process.

The Reaction Phase: Anticipating Your Reader's Responses

Writing presents you with a communication problem that doesn't generally arise when you're *speaking* to someone. The problem has to do with feedback: the feedback you receive when you converse with somebody, but have no way of receiving when you're writing. If you're speaking to somebody who doesn't understand or agree with a statement you've just made, he can let you know with a question, a challenging statement, a gesture, or an expression, and you can immediately address yourself to the response. You can rephrase your point in a different way, or intensify it with a remark like "No, I'm not kidding," or the ever popular "really."

Communicating with a reader, alas, deprives you of additional opportunity to get your point across, but it doesn't reduce the likelihood of a reader response that cries out for corrective action. What you write will occasionally surprise your reader or lead him to question the accuracy or fairness of your statements, and you can't simply *ignore* these reactions. You have to anticipate them and deal with them. If you don't, you'll break a communication circuit that is hard to maintain even under the best of circumstances.

In a variety of ways, and in ways you may not always be aware of, accomplished nonfiction writers are shrewdly anticipating the reactions of their readers.

Here's a slice of a *New York Times* editorial that illustrates the point:

Available now: 426 million pounds of butter, at 50 cents a pound below cost.

No, Sara Lee hasn't switched to margarine. The vendor

is Ronald Reagan, eager to rid government freezers of a surfeit of the high-priced spread. Trouble is, the only potential buyer is the Soviet Union.

How, you might ask, did the President slide into this embarrassment?

The sentence leading off the second paragraph ("No, Sara Lee . . .") employs a frequently used device: you imagine what your reader may be thinking. Likewise familiar is the device used in the third paragraph, in which you anticipate a reader's question by coming out and *asking* the question yourself.

Let's look at another example, this from a Lewis Thomas essay entitled "The Iks," from *Lives of a Cell:*

> The argument rests, of course, on certain assumptions about the core of human beings, and is necessarily speculative. You have to agree in advance that man is fundamentally a bad lot, out for himself alone, displaying such graces as affection and compassion only as learned habits. If you take this view, the story of the Iks can be used to confirm it. These people seem to be living together, clustered in small, dense villages, but they are really solitary, unrelated individuals with no evident use for each other. They talk, but only to make ill-tempered demands and cold refusals. They never sing. They turn the children out to forage as soon as they can walk, and desert the elders to starve whenever they can, and the foraging childen snatch food from the mouths of the helpless elders. It is a mean society.

The "of course" in the first sentence lets us know Thomas recognizes that while we probably don't need to have the assumption spelled out for us, we might find it interesting anyway. "Of course" anticipates—and forestalls—our thinking, "I already *know* that—why is he telling me?" Notice, too, how skillfully Thomas builds his argument. He is aware that the notion of man being a "fundamentally bad lot" is one that quite a few people—many readers, presumably—would agree with, so he keys his argument around this perception. Roughly half the paragraph consists of details which show that the Iks are *not* representative of other tribal societies.

Finally, an example from an article I wrote several years ago for *Playbill* on the celebrity tennis scene on Broadway:

> Before I go any further, a word of reassurance to those of you out there who, like me, could muddle through very nicely, thank you, without hearing so much as another syllable about celebrities who play tennis: this is not going to be another one of *those* articles. Elke Sommer is not going to materialize in a sexy pink tennis dress to rhapsodize about the gracefulness of Ilie Nastase. Lloyd Bridges is not going to surface and explain why he and a number of his tennis-playing colleagues are now playing for prize money in pro/celebrity competition. And Charlton Heston is not going to come down from the mountain to talk about his forehand.
>
> So stay with me. Yes, this is an article about celebrity tennis, but not the Hollywood brand of it. Our interest here is Broadway, and there is a difference.

I began the article this way because there had been a flood of publicity about celebrity tennis, and I figured that some readers might have had their fill of the subject. I built my opening around the possibility that my reader's first reaction might be, "Oh, no. Not another celebrity tennis article." And even after assuring the reader what he *wouldn't* find in this piece, I went even further: I came right out and asked the reader to "stay with me."

Was I being too paranoid? Perhaps. But given the choice between being overly paranoid and not being paranoid enough about your reader's responses, you're far better off, in my judgment, taking your paranoia to an extreme. And I don't think I'm alone in this view. One of the things you can't help noticing when you read accomplished writers is the number of phrases and statements that serve no other function than to make sure the reader and the writer are on the same wavelength. Here are the kinds of phrases I'm talking about:

"I can guess what you're thinking."

"As odd as it may seem . . ."

"Not surprisingly . . ."

"But that's another story and I'll get to it in a moment."

"I digress."

"It's hard to believe, but . . ."

"In other words . . ."

Don't underestimate the value of these phrases. They not only help to keep your reader's focus on the ideas and images that require his attention, they let him know that you're looking out for his welfare. As a result, he's likely to work a little harder than he otherwise might to make the writer/reader relationship flourish.

An Exercise in Reader Sensitivity

Now that you understand some general concepts of reader sensitivity, let's look at an example of writing in which reader sensitivity is noticeably lacking and let's see what we can do about building some sensitivity into the writing. In the following paragraph, the writer, a student, shows that he knows how to put together a sentence and that he has some interesting ideas to share. What he fails to do, however, is to assume enough control over the three key phases of the reading experience.

The first common mistake or habit I had to overcome as a bachelor in the supermarket was the mad dash for the steak section of the meat department. Most bachelors do this. I think this may be a carryover from pre-Cro-Magnon days. Remember, man does not live by red meat alone. If this word of advice doesn't slow your steps to the steaks and prime ribs, just check the prices carefully. Four (4) good-sized steaks are equal to a quarter-keg of Michelob. If you must eat like a caveman, at least comparison-shop for cheaper buys and cuts. At first, it may be difficult to control your saliva, but you'll find the time you spend really shopping is money in your pocket.

The problem starts with the first sentence. What does the writer want us to focus on—"a mistake" or "a habit"? They're not the same thing. What's more, the habit that the writer wants us to overcome isn't a "mad dash," it's *making* a mad dash. I know—"making" is understood. But by the writer, not necessarily by us.

Look at the second sentence. What does "this" at the end of the sentence refer to? The primary idea in the first sentence is "mistake" ("or habit"), so the logical referent for "this" would be mistake or habit. But the writer wants "this" to refer to "the mad dash." A false alarm.

I think this may be a carryover from pre-Cro-Magnon days. Remember, man does not live by red meat alone.

The "this" in the first sentence works okay, now that we know the reader is talking about a "mad dash for the steak section of the meat department." But the writer assumes "pre-Cro-Magnon days" alone is enough to convey the notion that our prehistoric ancestors lived largely on raw meat. I don't think it is. "Remember, man does not live by red meat alone" is a nice play on words, but it doesn't work.

The reason: the writer hasn't adequately prepared us for the shift into a tongue-in-cheek tone.

Let's go on.

> If this word of advice doesn't slow your steps to the steak and prime ribs, just check the prices carefully. Four (4) good-sized steaks are equal to a quarter-keg of Michelob.

What "word of advice" is the writer talking about? "Remember, man does not live by red meat alone" isn't really advice. It's a statement. "Four (4) good-sized steaks are equal to a quarter-keg of Michelob" is obviously meant to dramatize the high cost of steak. But why did the writer add the number 4 in parenthesis? And even though it's clear that the writer is referring to price, "are equal to" doesn't *say* price. The writer would have been better off saying simply, "Four good-sized steaks cost as much as a quarter-keg of Michelob."

> If you must eat like a caveman, at least comparison-shop for cheaper buys and cuts. At first it may be difficult to control your saliva, but you'll find the time you spend really shopping is money in your pocket.

The writer is saying basically this: if you insist on eating mainly beef, forget about steak and buy cheaper cuts. It might be hard for you to resist buying steak, but resisting the temptation will put more money in your pocket.

Trouble is, the words don't get these points across clearly enough. What does the writer mean, for example, by "comparison-shop"? Is he talking about going from one supermarket to another or simply going from one section of the meat department to another? (He's not controlling the association phase.) The phrase "control your saliva" bothers me, too. I have a vague idea of what the writer is trying to tell me—that when you're looking over the cheaper cuts of beef, it may be difficult to resist the steak—but I don't consider it my responsibility as a reader to *figure out* what the writer is trying to tell me.

How to correct these problems? Here's a reader-oriented revision.

> The first thing I had to do in order to become a better bachelor shopper was to break my habit of heading straight to the steak bin of the meat department as soon as I walked into the supermarket.

Here I come right out and tell the reader what this paragraph is going to be about.

> Most bachelors, I'm afraid, suffer from this same habit. It's a carryover, perhaps, from our pre-Cro-Magnon days, when a meal wasn't considered a meal unless it included plenty of raw meat.

I'm taking no chances here that my reader will not connect my reference to pre-Cro-Magnon days with the idea I want to get across—the notion (possibly humorous) that we may be genetically *drawn* to raw meat.

> But it may come as a shock to you bachelor shoppers that there are other things in the world to eat besides steak. Man does not live by steak alone.

I'm not crazy about the humor here, but at least I've set the reader up for the play on words in the second sentence by adopting a different tone in the first sentence.

> What's more, there are other types of beef to eat besides steak—almost all of them less expensive. Indeed one of the best reasons I can think of for developing a taste for food other than steak is price. In case you haven't looked recently, one good-sized steak costs as much as a six-pack of beer.

What I've done here is to relate the material to the reader's experience. In the original version, remember, the writer was comparing four (4) good-sized steaks to a quarter-keg of Michelob. But my guess is that most readers wouldn't know how much a keg of Michelob cost. Besides, we're talking about *bachelor* shopping. A bachelor would probably be more likely to buy *one* steak than four.

> Not that buying other food—even other expensive cuts of beef—may be easy for you to do if, like me, you'd be happier eating steak every day of the week.

Here I've simply anticipated a likely reader response—the fact that the reader might *like* steak.

> But take it from a veteran bachelor shopper: you can resist the temptation to buy steak, and develop a taste for other cuts of beef. And one of the first things you'll notice almost immediately when you start buying less steak is the amount of money in your pocket when you walk *out* of the supermarket. There will be more of it.

Again, the same idea. We're leaving little to the reader's imagination. We, the writer, are controlling what the reader is focusing on and processing.

Reader Sensitivity: Summing Up

I'm going to demonstrate my own reader sensitivity at this point by acknowledging the possibility that, in your view, I may have spent far too much time on this whole business of being sensitive to your reader's responses. As I suggested earlier, reader sensitivity is the one attribute, above all, that links today's most successful nonfiction writers and it is an essential ingredient of readability. All things being equal, a writer with mediocre technical skills but a high degree of reader sensitivity is more likely to succeed in commercial writing than a writer with great technical virtuosity but little or no sensitivity to his readers.

Exactly how you go about developing greater reader sensitivity is difficult to say. No aspect of writing I cover in my course is more difficult to teach than reader sensitivity. Before you can develop it, you have to recognize its importance. Then you have to be willing to sacrifice your own comfort and satisfaction as a writer in the interests of your reader.

Developing reader sensitivity takes time, so don't rush it. And don't get discouraged if trying to maintain an awareness of your reader inhibits your ability to write for a while. Work on each phase individually. Start by making sure you're communicating as *precisely* as possible. Get into the habit of reading aloud what you've written. (You might also consider reading what you've written into a tape recorder and playing it back.) If it doesn't read well aloud, it's probably not going to be easily absorbed by your reader.

Next, concentrate on the connecting phrase. Keep reminding yourself that your reader, unlike you, can't look two or three sentences ahead. Accept the fact that *everything*—yes, everything!—you feed your reader is going to trigger mental activity. Which means that everything you give your reader should have clear purpose behind it.

Finally, get into the habit of looking at your material, not as writer, but as somebody picking it up for the first time. It may seem hard at first, but you can train yourself to read what you've written from the perspective of somebody who is receiving this material for the first time. Be tough on yourself. Assume that the person who has written what you're reading is someone you neither like nor trust. Judge the material on the basis of the material itself. Is it clear? Can you believe it? Does it show a concern for the reader? All of this may not be much fun for you, but if you stay with it you will eventually find yourself doing automatically what you had to *think* about doing previously.

You'll begin to sense, not *after* you've written, but *as* you're writing, that you're not giving enough thought to your reader. More important, you'll know what to do about it, and care enough to do it.

3

Keeping Your Reader on the Track

MY friend Stan has an unusual skill: he's good at giving directions. He can tell you how to get from one place to another better than anybody I know.

What makes Stan so good at giving directions is that he doesn't simply drill them at you in that rapid-fire "go-down - three - lights - hang - a - left - you - can't - miss - it" gas-station-attendant style. No, Stan takes his time with you. He not only feeds you street names, route numbers, and left turns and right turns, but alerts you to landmarks along the way. And he'll interrupt his delivery every so often to satisfy himself that you are truly absorbing the directions and not simply nodding your head to be polite. "You know how to get to the Thruway, don't you?" he'll say. "Well, we're only about six minutes off of Exit 17. Exit 17 is the first exit right after the Norwalk tolls. Got that? The exit ramp will take you to a traffic light. At the light, you make a sharp left that will take you back *under* the Thruway. Now you're on Riverside Avenue—right?—which is Route 33, and you're heading north." Pause. "You with me? Good. You stay on Riverside for about a mile and a half, and you'll come to a big business intersection. At the intersection you'll see a Goodwill store on your right, and a big brown building across the street. That's the Post Road. . . ."

Stan makes his living as an electrical engineer, but if he

ever decided to become a professional writer, I suspect he'd make a go of it. True, he'd have to develop some basic writing skills—learn about leads and transitions and all the rest—but whatever he decided to write, you could count on one thing: he wouldn't lose many of his readers.

Reader-oriented writing consists largely of doing what my friend does so well, which is to get somebody—in this case, the reader—from one place to another without losing him en route. Your success in this enterprise will depend on any number of factors, all of which relate in one way or another to how coherently or engagingly you present your information. But your success will mainly depend on how carefully you control the direction and the intensity of your reader's focus.

When I talk about the reader's focus, I am talking mainly about whatever idea, image, or point the reader's mind happens to be resting on whenever a sentence ends. In other words, where your reader *is*. If your intention is to move your reader somewhere else (introduce a new point, etc.), you do your reader valuable service by *using that focal point as the connecting link to the next idea or image you're introducing*. Here's a brief example of what I'm talking about, from an E. B. White essay entitled "Riposte."

When a housewife, in New York or in Florida, comes home from market with a dozen eggs and opens her package, she finds twelve pure white eggs. This, to her, is not only what an egg should be, it is what an egg is. An egg is a white object. If this same housewife were to stray into New England and encounter a brown egg from the store, the egg would look somehow incorrect, wrong. It would look like something laid by a bird that didn't know what it was about. To a New Englander, the opposite is true (the opposite, obviously, of what looks wrong to an Easterner). Brought up as we are on the familiar beauty of a richly colored brown egg—gift of a Rhode Island Red or a Barred Plymouth Rock or a New Hampshire—when we visit New York and open a carton of chalk-white eggs, we are momentarily startled. Something is awry. The hen has missed fire. The eggs are white, therefore wrong.

This paragraph is about eggs—namely, the problem that some people have with brown eggs and other people have with white eggs. What should concern us, though, is how smoothly White guides our focus from one new point to the next. Let's look more closely.

> When a housewife, in New York or in Florida, comes home from the market with a dozen eggs and opens her package, she finds twelve pure white eggs. This, to her, is not only what an egg should be, it is what an egg is. An egg is a white object.

Our focus at the end of the first sentence is on the "twelve pure white eggs" the housewife in New York or Florida finds when she comes home from market and opens her egg container. The "this" in the second sentence keeps our focus on the eggs, but it also leads us to the *new* point of focus— "what an egg should be" and "what an egg is." "An egg"— the first two words in the next sentence —takes us from where we were to the new point—"a white object."

> If this same housewife were to stray into New England and encounter a brown egg from the store, the egg would look somehow incorrect, wrong. It would look like something laid by a bird that didn't know what it was about.

"If this same housewife" redirects our focus to the housewife mentioned in the first sentence, but connects her quickly to "brown egg" before introducing the new point— the fact that this housewife would think the brown egg looked "wrong." And "It would look like something laid by a bird . . ." is information that falls within the focal point of the last sentence.

> To a New Englander, the opposite is true . . . .

"Opposite" here refers directly back to the brown egg looking wrong.

> Brought up as we are on the familiar beauty of a richly colored brown egg—gift of a Rhode Island Red or a Barred Plymouth Rock or a New Hampshire—when we visit New York and open a carton of chalk-white eggs, we are momentarily startled.

"Brought up as we are" connects directly to "New Englander." It takes us to "richly colored brown egg"—a familiar focal point by now—and leads us logically to the next point: the fact that we are startled when we open a carton of chalk-white eggs.

> Something is awry. The hen has missed fire. The eggs are white, therefore wrong.

From "we are momentarily startled" we move to an explanation of why this is so—"Something is awry"—to the information that closes out the paragraph on the "theme" focal point—the eggs.

Getting the idea? Good. Now let's look at how Gay Talese directs the focus of his readers in a Frank Sinatra profile he wrote in the 1960s for *Esquire.*

> In some ways this quasi-family affair at a reserved table in a public place is the closest thing Sinatra now has to home life. Perhaps, having had a home and left it, this approximation is as close as he cares to come; although this does not seem precisely so because he speaks with such warmth about his family, keeps in close touch with his first wife, and insists that she make no decision without first consulting him. He is always eager to place his furniture or other mementoes of himself in her home or his daughter

Nancy's, and he also is on amiable terms with Ava Gardner. When he was in Italy making *Von Ryan's Express,* they spent some time together, being pursued wherever they went by the paparazzi. It was reported then that the paparazzi had made Sinatra a collective offer of $16,000, if he would pose with Ava Gardner; Sinatra was said to have made a counter offer of $32,000 if he could break one paparazzi arm and leg.

Our focus in this paragraph begins with a "quasi-private family affair at a reserved table." At the end of the paragraph our focus is on Sinatra making an offer of $32,000 to break one paparazzi arm and leg. Let's trace the route we take from beginning to end.

In some ways this quasi-family affair at a reserved table in a public place is the closest thing Sinatra now has to home life. Perhaps, having had a home and left it, this approximation is as close as he cares to come; although this does not seem precisely so because he speaks with such warmth about his family, keeps in close touch with his first wife, and insists that she make no decision without first consulting him.

Our focus at the end of the first sentence is on the idea that the "quasi-family affair at a reserved table in a public place" is the "closest thing Sinatra now has to home life." "This approximation" in the second sentence connects to the previous focus and serves as a link to the next idea— Sinatra's probable reasons for not having a home in the real sense of the term. Which, in turn, lets Talese offer additional material about Sinatra—his involvement with his first wife.

He is always eager to place his furniture or other mementoes of himself in her home or his daughter Nancy's, and he also is on amiable terms with Ava Gardner.

Because our focus was on Sinatra's involvement with his first wife, the following information—Sinatra's eagerness to place furniture, mementoes, etc., in his wife's or Nancy's place—flows logically. It also leads—logically, again—to Ava Gardner, who was Sinatra's second wife. Now our focus in on Ava Gardner.

> When he was in Italy making *Von Ryan's Express,* they spent time together, being pursued wherever they went by paparazzi.

From Ava Gardner herself, a new focus: Sinatra and Gardner being pursued by paparazzi.

> It was reported then that the paparazzi had made Sinatra a collective offer of $16,000, if he would pose with Ava Gardner; Sinatra was said to have made a counter offer of $32,000 if he could break one paparazzi arm and leg.

The focus route: from paparazzi, to the offer reportedly made by the paparazzi to Sinatra, and then to the counter offer. An easy journey by a solicitous tour guide.

Focus Control: A Closer Look

The principle we've been talking about throughout this chapter is easier to demonstrate than to explain. But basically it's a matter of structuring your sentences so that your reader doesn't have to scramble to keep pace with the *flow* of your ideas. In other words, you leave absolutely no doubt as to where you want your reader's focus to be.

In certain situations, the ideas and images themselves will provide the cues a reader needs to keep pace with any focus shifts. When you're dealing with narrative information, for instance, the natural progression of the narrative is usually enough to assure you that your reader's focus is where you want it. Look at the following *Newsweek* paragraph:

> When the long-awaited sound shrilled through her living room in Falls Church, Va., at 2:39 a.m., Pat Lee was afraid to pick up the phone. A neighbor answered, passed the receiver—and the tension dissolved in a babble of endearments and marital badinage. "I'm OK, I'm OK, I'm OK," she burbled to her husband, 37-year-old administrative officer Gary Earl Lee. Gently she chided him for the meager three-line message he'd sent at Christmas—her first since a twelve-line note in early summer. Quietly, he explained that he had been frequently shifted, blindfolded, around the country and had spent the last six months in solitary confinement.

We have little trouble keeping pace here because in narrative, there is a logical sequence to the material. You don't have to tie "a neighbor answered" to the previous focal point—"Pat Lee was afraid to pick up the phone"—because the idea itself produces the appropriate shift in focus.

Neither is there generally a need for such devices when you're writing the kind of directions that normally appear in "how-to" pieces, as we see in this brief section from the late Richard Gehman's book, *The Haphazard Gourmet*. Here Gehman offers his instructions on how to make great chili.

> Sauté about two pounds of ground beef, the cheaper the better, and a pound of ground fresh pork, in the grease or oil of your choice. Throw in three onions about the size of shrunken heads from South American Indians (this recipe can get expensive, for you may have to go to South America and buy a shrunken head to find out how big one is). Put in two green peppers, or three or four hot red Italian peppers. Onions and peppers must be finely chopped, of course. Let all this go on a low heat for about a half-hour. Now chop in five tomatoes, seeds and all . . .

Again, as in the *Newsweek* paragraph, connecting devices are unnecessary because the focus shifts are implicitly controlled. We know that you don't have to throw in the three onions until *after* you've completed the first step, and that the peppers follow the onions. Gehman doesn't have to tell us.

But in other types of writing, particularly in expository writing, the lack of connecting devices often produces a choppy reading experience. Here's a student example that shows you what I mean.

> Polls, the staples of campaign coverage, are one example of how people are manipulated and influenced to think a certain way. People fail to realize that polls overemphasize the leads and gains of the candidates and that dramatic changes occur daily depending on incidents influenced by campaigners. Voter sentiment can be temporarily won by an incident or statement, and campaigners know this. Remember, campaigners excel in view of how we interpret them.

Our focus here is initially on polls and what they exemplify. But it shifts abruptly in the second sentence to what "people fail to realize." True, there is a mention of "people" in the first sentence, but the mention is buried in the middle of the sentence. Similarly, the focus jump that takes us to "voter sentiment" in the third sentence catches us by surprise, even though we're talking about voters. The final focus shift that takes us from "campaigners know this" to a warning that we should beware of their tactics is no smoother. So as readers we've been forced to scramble in order to keep pace with the writer.

Here's a revision in which we convey the same ideas but through an easier-to-follow route.

> Polls, the staples of campaign coverage, are one example of how people are manipulated and influenced to think a

certain way. Many people, for instance, look at the results of polls and assume these numbers are an accurate reflection of voter sentiment. But what these people fail to realize is that the numbers can be misleading: instead of reflecting *true* voter sentiment they may simply be reflecting voter response to a particular statement by a campaigner or an incident that has been orchestrated by a campaigner for no other reason than to influence the outcome of a poll. Campaigners, after all, recognize that their standing in a poll could, in and of itself, be a factor in attracting votes, and so they tend more and more to plan their campaign strategy around the *timing* of polls.

This revision is far from perfect but at least we've given the paragraph a sense of unity. The unifying thread throughout the first three sentences is "people," and "people" takes us logically to "campaigners." The information in the revision is essentially the same as it is in the original, but the ride through the paragraph is smoother.

Here's another example in which a student writer's failure to control reader focus forces the reader to reorient his focus almost line by line.

The theater honors its outstanding members in various areas relating to the theater each year. This coveted honor is presented through the Tony Awards. The ceremony for this year was on Sunday, June 7. Some of the categories honored are: acting, stage design, music, directing, and lighting. Each category is presented with announcing the individuals nominated for that category and then announcing the winner. This year's best musical play went to *42nd Street*.

The problems in this paragraph go beyond focus control, but let's stick to focus. Trouble begins in the second sentence, where the writer introduces "this coveted honor" without having mentioned any specific honor in the first sentence. Our focus at the end of the second sentence is on

"Tony Awards," which is not quite the same thing as "This ceremony," the phrase that introduces the third sentence. The information in the fourth sentence isn't logically connected to the focal point—Sunday, June 7—that ended the third sentence.

We can remedy some of the problems in this paragraph by selecting a single focus point and by *channeling all the information through the same focus.* Here's how the paragraph reads when we use this technique with the word "year."

> Each year, the theater honors its outstanding members in various areas relating to the theater in a ceremony known as the Tony Awards. This year's Tony Awards ceremony was held on Sunday, June 7, and as in past years, the chief categories honored were acting, music, directing, design setting, and lighting. Once again, as in past years, each award was presented by first announcing the nominees and then the winner. The Tony Award for the best musical play this year went to *42nd Street.*

What have we done here? We've simply used "year" as a technical device for controlling the reader's focus. Here's the same technique illustrated in a Nora Ephron essay entitled "On Consciousness Raising." Notice how the focus stays primarily on the same point throughout—on the consciousness raising group. Notice, too, how almost every bit of information Ms. Ephron gives us in this paragraph is tied, one way or another, to this focal point. I've italicized the prime focal points throughout.

> My *consciousness raising group* is still going on. Every Monday night *it* meets, somewhere in Greenwich Village, and *it* drinks a lot of red wine and eats a lot of cheese. A friend of mine who is in *it* tells me that at the *last meeting,* each of the women took her turn to explain, in considerable detail, what she was planning to stuff her Thanksgiving

turkey with. I no longer go to the *group,* for a variety of reasons, the main one being that I don't think the process works. Well, let me put that less dogmatically and explicitly —*this particular group* did not work for me. I don't mean that I wasn't able to attain the exact goal I set for myself: in the six months I spent in *the group,* my marriage went through an incredibly rough period. But that's not what I mean when I say it didn't work.

Putting the Technique to Work

Most accomplished writers control the focus of their readers almost routinely, but *student* writers I've come across go to the *opposite* extreme. Not only do student writers fail to continually reinforce the main focus, they rarely use a reference to this main thought as a vehicle for introducing new ideas and images. What they do, instead, is simply rattle off details without any sense of how the reader is absorbing and consolidating these details. Here's an example.

> Advertising has been known to create and sustain a market. A prime example of this is what advertising has done for designer blue jeans. Seventy-five percent of designer jeans advertising can be seen on television at any hour of the day across the nation. Since this advertising has begun, status jeans have taken over 17 percent of the jean market and sales have been estimated at wholesale $1 billion last year. What has sustained this business is advertising, some of the worst advertising ever—where the emphasis is on the derrière, those snug jeans hugging the wearer's behind.

There is useful information here, but the section doesn't communicate readably. Part of the reason is that there are numerous grammatical problems, but the main reason this section doesn't communicate effectively is that the writer isn't sensitive enough to what we as readers are focusing on and how sharp this focus is. Let's look at the section in detail.

> Advertising has been known to create and sustain a market. A prime example of this is what advertising has done for designer blue jeans.

A promising, if not terribly imaginative, start. The writer directs our focus to advertising's ability to "create and sustain a market." He eases our attention smoothly to the manner in which advertising has done "this" for designer jeans.

> Seventy-five percent of designer jeans advertising can be seen on television at any hour of the day across the nation. Since this advertising has begun, status jeans have taken over 17 percent of the jean market and sales have been estimated at wholesale $1 billion last year.

The writer is now beginning to build his case, to present information designed to show how advertising's effect on designer jeans exemplifies the power of advertising "to create and sustain a market."

But consider the focus shift. At the end of the second sentence, our focus was on "what advertising has done for designer blue jeans." The next sentence—"Seventy-five percent of designer jeans advertising can be seen," etc.— doesn't say anything about what advertising has *done,* it simply states a fact *about* designer jeans advertising. Something is missing. The writer has asked us to shift focus but hasn't oriented us in any specific direction. Had the writer recognized that our focus at the end of the second sentence had indeed been on what advertising has *done* for designer jeans, he would have introduced his new information within the context of this focus. For example:

> A prime example of this is what advertising has done for designer blue jeans. If you watch much television, you've undoubtedly noticed that advertisements for status jeans have become almost as ubiquitous as station announcements. Since this advertising . . .

True, we haven't shown as yet what advertising "has done" for designer jeans, but we'll do this shortly. The important thing is we've shepherded the reader's focus from the general idea of what "advertising has done," etc., to the vehicle —television—with which we intend to prove our point. Now the reader is ready for television-related data which will connect to the main point of the passage.

Let's go back to the original:

> What has sustained this business is advertising, some of the worst advertising ever—where the emphasis is on the derrière, those snug jeans hugging the wearer's behind.

Look back at the original paragraph. Notice that at the end of the third sentence, our focus is on the gains that status jeans have made through advertising—the 17 percent share of the jean market; the $1 billion in wholesale sales. Early in the next sentence, however, the writer directs our focus to "this business"—in "what has sustained this business"—which is not a precise enough representation of what the writer wants to get across. What's more, the writer has already advanced the point that advertising sells jeans, so why repeat it? The writer, we can assume, is now anxious to make known his feelings about the quality of this advertising, which means, of course, yet another focus shift for the reader. But the shift is difficult. Here is what might have worked better.

> . . . sales have been estimated at $1 billion wholesale a year. It's true, of course, that some of this advertising, with the emphasis on the derrière, those snug jeans hugging the

wearer's behind, hasn't established any new standards of good taste in advertising, but nobody ever said you had to be tasteful in the U.S. to make money. In the meantime . . .

The writer's feelings about the quality of the status jeans advertising don't directly relate to the main point here, which, remember, is the power of advertising to "create and sustain a market." So it is up to the writer, if he is going to inject these asides, to make it clear that this information is indeed parenthetical and subjective. This is what we accomplish with "It's true, of course." And it is also up to the writer, once he's let his own feelings be known, to get the reader back to the main point again. Which we do with the phrase "In the meantime."

So much for a student example of failing to exercise enough control over the reader's focus. The following paragraph comes from a piece published in a national magazine. It's a better written paragraph than the one we've just gone over, but it suffers from many of the same focus-jump problems.

Counting on the fingers might be considered the ultimate in back to basics. Ancient civilizations, from the Egyptians and the Romans in the West to the Chinese in the East, had systems for doing calculations on their fingers, as did the American Indians. The reason we have a ten-"digit" number system is that we have ten fingers (anthropologists have located a few societies that have five-based systems, presumably because their first mathematician had only one arm). The Venerable Bede, an English historian and monk, writing in the late seventh century, described in detail one system in which the left hand represents the numbers 1 to 99, with 1 to 9 formed by the little finger, the ring finger and the middle finger, and the tens by the thumb and forefinger. Indeed, the English words "eleven" and "twelve" derive from finger counting and mean "one left" and "two left" after using up the ten fingers. But for some reason, in modern times, the First Commandment of learning math has always been: Do it in your head.

This isn't badly written at all. The information is solid. The language is accessible. And you can't help but like a writer who lightens up a dry and not terribly exciting subject with touches of humor. But the paragraph would have worked much better had the writer been more careful about controlling the reader's focus. Here's what I mean:

> Counting on the fingers might be considered the ultimate in back to basics. Ancient civilizations, from the Egyptians and Romans in the West to the Chinese in the East, had systems for doing calculations on their fingers, as did the American Indians.

The first sentence is fine. Notice, though, that we are sixteen words into the second sentence before we know exactly where to direct our focus. "Back to basics"—our focus at the end of the first sentence—doesn't readily connect to the material at the beginning of the second sentence. It's not until we get to "had systems for doing calculations on their fingers" that we know exactly where we are. Letting a reader out of your sight for sixteen words is a risk few careful writers would ever take. Here's how a more focus-oriented writer would have handled the same information.

> Counting on the fingers might be considered the ultimate in back to basics. After all, the practice of finger-calculating dates back to ancient civilizations, to the Egyptians and Romans in the West and to the Chinese in the East. Even the American Indians counted on their fingers.

"After all" tells the reader immediately that the incoming information is going to back up the previous sentence. "The practice of doing finger-calculating," coming this early in the sentence, further sharpens focus. The reader now has no problem connecting the information that comes later. In the original version, the reader is *first* handed a piece of information and *then* told what to do with it. In the revision, we tell the reader how to sort the information *before* we give it to him. Let's go on.

> The reason we have a ten-"digit" number system is that we have ten fingers (anthropologists have located a few societies that have five-based systems, presumably because their first mathematician had only one arm).

The information within the parenthesis is a nice touch, and I wouldn't want to get rid of it. But in the original version, the reader's focus at the end of the second sentence is on the general point of the paragraph—the fact that counting on your fingers has to be considered the ultimate in back to basics. Once again, the writer introduces a new point—"The reason we have a ten-'digit' number system"—without leading our focus there. Here's a revision that corrects the problem.

> The fact that we have ten fingers, in fact, may explain our ten-"digit" number system (anthropologists, etc.).

"In fact," midway in the sentence, intensifies focus. "The fact that we have ten fingers" connects directly to the reader's present focal point and leads him easily to the new one—our "ten-'digit' number system."

The focus problem worsens in the next sentence of the original.

> The Venerable Bede, an English historian and monk, writing in the late seventh century, described in detail one system in which the left hand represents the numbers 1 to 99, with 1 to 9 formed by the little finger, the ring finger and the middle finger, and the tens by the thumb and forefinger.

Solid information, nicely presented. But the previous focal point, remember, was "ten-'digit' number system"—and in this sentence there is no *direct* reference to a "ten-'digit' number system." It is implied, but obliquely. The writer is tying together the idea of counting on the fingers with the ten-digit system, but we don't really know what he is up to until we've finished the sentence. In other words, the writer has temporarily disoriented us—again.

The writer could have spared the reader this inconvenience. All he had to do was add a simple sentence which would say, in effect, this is what I want you to focus on. Something like:

> Finger counting has produced some fairly elaborate mathematical systems.

Now our focus is on "mathematical systems." The "Venerable Bede" can follow as is; this time the reader has a much easier time absorbing and sorting the information.

Let's look at the next sentence, keeping in mind that our focus is on the system described by Bede in which three fingers represent the numbers from 1 to 99.

> Indeed, the English words "eleven" and "twelve" derive from finger counting and mean "one left" and "two left" after using up ten fingers.

"Indeed" intensifies reader focus. But our focus wasn't on "the English words 'eleven' and 'twelve.' " We haven't even been introduced to this information yet. Our focus is on Bede's system; moreover, as the rest of the sentence shows, the writer wants to leave Bede's system and get back to finger counting in general. Here's what a simple shifting of phrases can do to rectify the problem:

> Bede apart, the English words "eleven" and "twelve" derive from finger counting and mean "one left" and "two left" after using up ten fingers.

"Bede apart," unlike "indeed," alerts the reader to a *new* piece of information and tells us to forget about Bede and move our focus forward.

Back to the conclusion of the original version:

> But for some reason, in modern times, the First Commandment of learning math has always been: Do it in your head.

More problems. The writer throughout this paragraph has been building a case for finger counting. The last sentence is clearly meant to show how silly it is, given everything that has happened in history, to condemn people who count on their fingers. The thought is a nice idea, but the writer doesn't make his point smoothly. Why? Because the focus change is too abrupt. The writer hasn't sufficiently primed us for the change. What's needed here is something on the order of:

> Yet, in spite of finger counting's long and noble tradition, in spite of its importance to the civilizations of the Romans, the Egyptians, the Chinese, in spite of its role in inspiring elaborate mathematical systems, and in spite of its impact on our language, the First Commandment of learning math in modern times is: Don't do it on your fingers.

I know. We're repeating ourselves here. The reader has already been told about ancient civilizations and elaborate mathematical systems and the rest. But if the final sentence is going to carry any punch, we have to redirect, very briefly, the reader's focus to the points we've raised throughout this paragraph, so that the contrast doesn't fall flat. The writer doesn't do this.

Go back to pages 52–53 and reread the paragraph as it originally was written. Then read this rewrite, in which the only thing we've done is to take more responsibility for the reader's focus.

Counting on the fingers might be considered the ultimate in back to basics. After all, the practice of doing finger-calculating dates back to ancient civilizations—to the Egyptians and Romans in the West, and to the Chinese in the East. Even the American Indians counted on their fingers. Indeed, the fact that we have ten fingers may explain our ten-"digit" number system (anthropologists have located a few societies that have five-based systems, presumably because their first mathematician had only one arm).

Rudimentary though it is, finger counting has produced some fairly elaborate mathematical systems. One such system is described in detail by the Venerable Bede, an English historian and monk, in the seventh century. In this system, the left hand represents the numbers 1 to 99, with the 1 to 9 formed by the little finger, the ring finger, and the middle finger, and the tens by the thumb and forefinger. Bede apart, the English words "eleven" and "twelve" derive from finger counting and mean "one left" and "two left" after using up ten fingers.

Yet, in spite of finger counting's long and noble tradition, in spite of its importance to the civilizations of the Romans, the Egyptians, the Chinese, in spite of its role in inspiring elaborate mathematical systems, and in spite of its impact on the English language, the First Commandment of learning math in modern times is: Don't do it on your fingers.

So much for a writer who doesn't seem to care whether we keep pace with him or not. One writer who does care a great deal is John Gregory Dunne, a novelist, screen writer, and essayist whose ability to control the responses and the focus of his readers is such that I had to read the following paragraph at least a half-dozen times in order to examine the paragraph with a purely analytic eye. I'll use the paragraph to close out this chapter because I've seen few other passages that better dramatize how controlling your reader's focus can contribute to your writing effectiveness.

Quintana will be eleven this week. She approaches adolescence with what I can only describe as panache, but then watching her journey from infancy has always been like watching Sandy Koufax pitch or Bill Russell play basketball. There is the same casual arrogance, the implicit sense that no one has ever done it any better. And yet it is difficult for a father to watch a daughter grow up. With each birthday she becomes more like us, an adult, and what we cling to is the memory of the child. I remember the first time I saw her in the nursery at Saint John's Hospital. It was after visiting hours and my wife and I stood staring through the soundproof glass partition at the infants in their cribs, wondering which was ours. Then a nurse in a surgical mask appeared from a back room carrying a fierce, black-haired baby with a bow in her hair. She was just seventeen hours old and her face was still wrinkled and red and the identification beads on her wrist had not our name but only the letters "NI." "NI" stood for "No Information," the hospital's code for an infant to be placed for adoption. Quintana is adopted.

"Quintana will be eleven this week": a simple statement that gets our focus on somebody—we don't know as yet who this somebody is—whose name is Quintana and who is approaching an eleventh birthday.

She approaches adolescence with what I can only describe as panache, but then watching her journey from infancy has always been like watching Sandy Koufax pitch or Bill Russell play basketball.

"She [Quintana] approaches adolescence" picks up our focus right where it was when the first sentence ended. "With what I can only describe as panache" introduces the first-person writer and primes us for new information: what it is about Quintana that has made watching her journey from infancy like "watching Sandy Koufax pitch or Bill Russell play basketball." Dunne wastes no time giving data related to this new idea. But notice that while he is creating new focal points—the way Sandy Koufax pitches and the way Bill Russell plays basketball—he is quick to connect these bits of information with his focus idea: Quintana turning eleven. He does this with the phrase "her journey from infancy." Look what would have happened had those four words been left out.

> She approaches adolescence with what I can only describe as panache, but then watching her has always been like watching Sandy Koufax pitch or Bill Russell play basketball.

Granted, the overall meaning of this sentence is not drastically affected by this omission. But the phrase "watching her" raises the question "watching her do *what?*" The omission also upsets the balance of the sentence: Without "journey from infancy," the references to Koufax and Russell lose impact. So even though the meaning is not lost, in that fraction of a millisecond we lose touch with the writer.

> There is the same casual arrogance, the implicit sense that no one has ever done it any better.

This sentence, again, starts right where our focus is—on how Sandy Koufax pitched and Bill Russell played basketball, and what these things have to do with Quintana turning eleven, growing up. Most of the writers I have had in my class, had they written this piece, would have omitted this sentence, they would have figured that comparing Quintana's growing up with Koufax's way of pitching or Bill Russell's style on the court was enough to reinforce the idea of "panache." But to leave out the added information is to risk the possibility that the reader's perception of how Koufax pitched and how Russell played basketball may differ from what the writer had in mind. Now we can close the file on "panache," and on Koufax and Russell as well.

> And yet it is difficult for a father to watch a daughter grow up.

A new direction here, but one we can easily follow because Dunne, ever the careful giver of directions, alerts us to the change. The word "yet" does it. But he doesn't just point us in a new direction, he gives us a connection—"to watch a daughter grow up"—which takes us from where our focus has already been (Quintana becoming eleven) to where he now wants it to go: on a father responding to a daughter's growing up. What's more, this statement primes us for what's to come. We want to know *why* it is difficult for a father to watch a daughter grow up.

> With each birthday she becomes more like us, an adult, and what we cling to is the memory of the child.

With this sentence, Dunne answers the question in the previous sentence—why it's difficult for a father to watch a daughter growing up. Notice, again, the use of a connecting phrase, "With each birthday," to take our focus from where it was to where Dunne wants it.

> I remember the first time I saw her in the nursery at Saint John's Hospital.

A new piece of information but easily sorted because "memory of the child" in the previous sentence connects to "I remember the first time" and to "birthday" as well. Now our focus is on Dunne in the nursery.

> It was after visiting hours and my wife and I stood staring through the soundproof glass partition at the infants in their cribs, wondering which was ours.

"It was after visiting hours" intensifies our focus. It gives us a detail plugged into "the first time I saw her in the nursery." But here's a curious piece of information—"my wife and I stood staring through the soundproof glass partition at the infants . . . wondering which was ours." This raises a question. Why would Dunne—not to mention his wife—not know which infant was theirs? And what is his wife doing up and about so quickly after the delivery?

> Then a nurse in a surgical mask appeared from a back room carrying a fierce, black-haired baby with a bow in her hair. She was just seventeen hours old and her face was still wrinkled and red and the identification beads on her wrist had not our name but only the letters "NI."

"Then" guides our focus—that part of our focus, at any rate, that isn't still pondering the mystery of why the parents don't know who their child is. The baby arrives, and we know where to file the details—all except for that last one, the business about the letters "NI." We're now primed to receive information that will tell us what the letters mean. And we receive it.

> "NI" stood for "No Information," the hospital's code for an infant to be placed for adoption. Quintana is adopted.

To be sure, this passage engages us for reasons that go beyond Dunne's ability to keep our focus under control. There is a comfortable rhythm to the sentences. The tone is appropriate to the material. And Dunne doesn't simply *tell* us what it was like there at the hospital, he *shares* the experience with us by giving us concrete details: he and his wife standing at the nursery window, the infant "fierce, black-haired . . . with a bow in her hair" being carried in. And the allusions to Sandy Koufax and Bill Russell—they help, too. The freshness of the analogy—comparing a child's journey from infancy with the style of an athlete— is Dunne's way of helping us *enjoy* the trip all the more.

Ultimately, though, the reason this paragraph works so

well—and by "works" I mean it takes us where Dunne wants us to go with pleasure and with ease—is that Dunne is a superb tour guide. He doesn't let us out of his sight for a moment.

4

Staging:
A New Approach
to Clarity

CLARITY is so elemental a consideration in writing that to single it out as simply one aspect of the process seems almost silly, rather like offering as part of a cooking school curriculum a course on how to make food taste good. Far from being simply a rudimentary skill you master early in your career in order to move more quickly into the more "creative" and "imaginative" aspects of writing, clarity is the very essence of the craft. It could be argued, in fact, that if you haven't conveyed your ideas or images clearly to your reader, you haven't really *written* anything, you've simply put a lot of words on paper.

But its importance apart, clarity is probably more difficult to teach than any other single facet of writing, and it is especially difficult to delineate the specific techniques that produce it. And with good reason. For apart from the obvious mechanical considerations (knowing how to spell and punctuate, etc.), clarity in writing is more a function of how clearly and logically you *organize* your thoughts—a conceptual skill—than of how clearly and logically you *express* these thoughts—a "writing" skill. Indeed, if your thoughts aren't well organized, it doesn't matter how large or varied your vocabulary is, how vivid an imagination you have, or how lyrically you compose a sentence; your writing, more often than not, will puzzle your readers. People may admire the way you "use words," but hardly anybody will read you.

Some Thoughts about Thoughts

We all learned in grammar school that a sentence is a group of words expressing a complete thought. Unfortunately, most of us have been conditioned in our writing to think more about *words* than about *thoughts*. Consequently, when most people write they are primarily concerned with *how* they express themselves rather than with *what* they're expressing or—more important, perhaps— with whether they are reaching their readers.

Take a look at the following sentence, from a magazine advertisement for Hughes Aircraft:

> A structural and thermal test model of NASA's Galileo Probe is undergoing a series of tests simulating every environment that the Hughes-built probe will experience from launch through descent into the Jovian atmosphere in the late 1980s.

Grammatically, this sentence is virtually perfect. Even a trigger-happy editor would have trouble eliminating excess verbiage from it. But if you can absorb all the information in this sentence in one reasonably quick reading, you're smarter than I am. Sure, you can *read* the sentence easily enough, but how many of the ideas in it make any impact? Not many, I think. The ideas in this sentence come at you too quickly. The sentence suffers from what I like to call "idea overload."

Let's be fair. Someone who works for NASA or Hughes or is familiar with the U.S. space program could probably process the information in this sentence fairly quickly and easily. He already knows that there is such an animal as a Galileo Probe—you don't have to tell him what it is. He knows, in all likelihood, that the mission of this probe is to go to Jupiter in the late 1980s (and probably knows that "Jovian" refers to Jupiter), and that Hughes built it. So the only "new" idea the mind of such a person is obliged to process is the fact that a structural and thermal model of this vehicle is undergoing a series of tests to see how the probe is going to fare in the various environments it will encounter during the actual journey.

On the other hand, for somebody who has never heard of the Galileo Probe (and, remember, this ad was written for the general public), virtually everything in this sentence is new and unfamiliar. Consider the individual units of information a reader has to process in this sentence before the meaning of the sentence is clear.

1. NASA has a new space probe named Galileo (we're assuming here that most readers know what NASA is).

2. There is a test model of this probe.

3. The model is "structural" and "thermal," which is to say it has the same structural and heat-resistant properties as the real thing.

4. Hughes Aircraft is building the probe and presumably built the model as well.

5. The probe is going to fly to the "Jovian atmosphere" (i.e., to Jupiter) in the late 1980s.

6. The tests the probe is undergoing are designed to simulate the environments the probe will experience during its journey.

It's asking a lot of *any* reader to absorb (forget about retain) all of this information in a single sentence. There's simply too much of it. If you want to make absolutely certain your reader absorbs the information in the above sentence, you have to allow the reader sufficient space and time to absorb each thought. You have to make sure your reader's brain is "ready" to receive a particular thought before you ask him to process it. You have, in effect, to spoonfeed the reader, seeing to it that no new piece of information gets introduced until the *previous* bit has been chewed, swallowed and, to stretch the point, digested. Here's how this approach might work with the sentence from the Hughes ad.

> The National Aeronautics and Space Agency of the United States (NASA) has a new space vehicle. It's called the Galileo Probe and it's being built by Hughes Aircraft. The plans are to launch the probe into the atmosphere of Jupiter in the late 1980s, but NASA is now working with a test model of it. The model is made of the same structural materials as the probe and has the same heat-resistance characteristics. The tests now going on are enabling NASA officials to see how the probe will withstand the various environments it will encounter during its journey to Jupiter.

I know. This sounds like something you might read in a second-grade primer—"Look at Dick and Jane (and Spot) standing near the space probe." We've oversimplified, perhaps (let's call it idea *underload*). Then again, when you're dealing with material a reader is likely to find unfamiliar, you're better off erring to this extreme than to the opposite extreme exemplified by the original paragraph.

But we don't have to limit ourselves to options in the extreme. There's a middle ground here, a balance between feeding your reader too much in too short a time and feeding him too little too slowly. Let's have a go at it:

> A test model of the Galileo Probe—the new NASA space vehicle being built by Hughes to fly to Jupiter in the late 1980s—is currently undergoing a series of simulated flights. The purpose of these flights is to determine if the probe is sufficiently strong and heat-resistant to withstand the environmental pressure it will encounter during its journey from launch to descent into the Jovian atmosphere.

What we've done here is to *stage* the information; organize it in a way that gives it readability and makes it more easily accessible to the reader. In the first sentence we introduce the reader to the Galileo Probe, tell him what it is, and then tell him what makes it worth mentioning: the fact that it's undergoing a series of simulated flights, etc. In the second sentence (having already told the reader what we're talking about), we tell him the purpose of the flights. So, even though we're conveying to the reader a good deal of information in these two sentences, we're actually asking him to absorb only two general thoughts: (1) what the Galileo Probe is doing, and (2) why it's doing it.

To organize information with an eye toward readability and impact—this is what you do when you *stage* your material rather than simply *write* it. Staging takes the concept of clarity beyond the need simply to make yourself *understood* when you write. Implicit in the staging concept are: (1) there are degrees of clarity; and (2) there is a difference between the meaning of a thought and the impact of that thought.

So, when you think about staging, you begin to see that the essence of writing is not so much how cleverly or imaginatively you use words but how logically and strategically you orchestrate your thoughts. That is why I'm going to talk very little in this chapter about words, and why I will be concentrating almost entirely on the thoughts these words represent—and how your ability to stage these thoughts to meet your reader's needs is the essence of writing with clarity.

The Basics of Staging

The staging techniques we'll be looking into in this chapter are all rooted, in one way or another, in two general principles regarding thoughts and images. These principles, which go beyond the specific meaning of these thoughts and images concern (1) the relative importance of the thoughts and images, and (2) their function in your overall presentation. Let's look a little more closely at both aspects, and how they relate to staging.

Importance: Setting Priorities

At its most rudimentary level, writing is essentially a decision-making process: deciding which thoughts and images best convey certain information; deciding which words and which presentation of these words best communicate these thoughts and images. And as in any decision-making process, you have to set priorities.

There's no need to get bogged down in theory here. Look at the following paragraph:

> Kelsey was elected mayor in 1976. His corrupt administration was exposed in a series of newspaper articles three years later, and he was forced to resign.

Strictly speaking, there is nothing wrong with the way this short paragraph is written. But reread the second sentence with the following question in mind: what is the most important thought in this sentence? The answer, based on the way the sentence is constructed, is the fact that Kelsey was forced to resign because of the newspaper articles that exposed his corrupt regime. Now look at this revision:

> Kelsey was elected mayor in 1976. His administration, however, was filled with corruption, and three years later, after a series of newspaper articles revealed he was receiving kickbacks from a building contractor, he was forced to resign.

The information here is the same as in the previous example, but not the emphasis. Here the main thought is that

Kelsey's administration was filled with corruption; the fact that he was forced to resign because of the series of newspaper articles is of lesser importance. The difference between the two examples, of course, is that in the first the fact of corruption is expressed in the phrase "corrupt administration"; the idea is conveyed by the adjective "corrupt." In the second example, the idea is expressed more prominently: "His administration, however, was filled with corruption. . . ." Thus the reader is likely to attach more importance to the notion of corruption in the second example than in the first.

Now for the critical question: what was the *writer's* intent? Did he want to emphasize the newspaper's role in destroying Kelsey's reputation? If so, then the first example does the job. But if corruption was indeed the main point the writer wanted to get across, then the first example falls short. Why? Because there the writer failed to give corruption the prominence it deserves.

The point to bear in mind here—and it's a point I'll be elaborating on in a moment—is that your presentation (i.e., staging) should always reflect the relative importance you attach to each thought you present. I'll get to a few techniques that relate to this relationship between importance and presentation shortly, but now let's look at the second basic principle that underlies staging—the *function* of thoughts and images.

Function: Thoughts in Action

Look at the following two sentences:

Friday was one of the hottest days in memory. It was so hot that the interstate highway buckled in several places, snarling traffic for miles.

Both sentences convey the same general thought—the fact that it was extremely hot on Friday. But each sentence serves a different function. The first introduces the reader to a piece of information that presumably is new to him. The second reinforces the thought.

Now consider these two sentences:

> I want to tell you about Friday. First of all, it was one of the hottest days I can ever remember—so hot that the interstate highway buckled in several places, snarling traffic for miles.

In this example, we combine in the second sentence the two functions served by the two sentences in the previous example: a new idea is introduced and reinforced. But the first sentence serves neither of these functions: it doesn't really provide information: it simply sets the reader up for the thoughts to come. In other words, it serves a priming function.

In and of itself, being aware of what function a thought or an idea serves within a sentence or a paragraph is of limited value. But when you combine an awareness of a thought's function with an awareness of its importance, you have a basis for effective staging. Important thoughts and images, for instance, need to be staged with their importance in mind, and may well require reinforcement by other thoughts. Thoughts of lesser importance, on the other hand, should serve an essentially *supportive* function. *The basic function of staging is to make sure that important thoughts receive the prominence they deserve and that they are supported by back-up thoughts to maximize their impact.*

One approach I use in my class to help students organize their thinking is to divide thoughts into three broad categories, based on their importance and their function:

1. *Umbrella Thoughts.* The general, or core, ideas you're trying to get across in any presentation.

2. *Big Thoughts*. Specific ideas or images that fall within the realm of umbrella thoughts and serve to reinforce, clarify, or elaborate upon the umbrella thoughts.

3. *Little Thoughts*. Ideas or images whose chief function is to reinforce big thoughts.

There is a fourth category of thoughts that I am not terribly concerned with in this chapter. This category includes ideas or images not related to the material but to the reader's attention and interest. Their general purpose is to help keep the reader on track and interested in the material.

Above all, the one thing I'd like you to keep in mind as we cover the concepts in this chapter is that there is a difference between the thought you express and the words you use to express the thought. The same thought can be expressed in any number of ways—some ways, obviously, more effective than others. But the measure of effectiveness is not the cleverness of the words you use but the clarity and the impact of the thoughts expressed in these words. If you learn nothing else from this chapter—indeed from this book—let it be the importance of focussing your mental energy primarily on the thoughts you want to get across and secondarily on the words you use to express these thoughts.

Umbrella Thoughts and How They Can Help You Write More Clearly

A basic principle of staging your material is knowing at all times what you're trying to say. No snickering, please. One problem that I find frequently in the student papers I receive weekly is that my students get so caught up in what they are trying to write, they lose sight of what they are trying to say. In the process, they lose the only person they're writing for—me.

Here's a brief sample from a writer who is presenting a good deal of information without being sure of what he wants to say, which explains why the paragraph seems muddled.

> The corporate business jet industry is growing at a fast rate. This industry concept, developed by Bill Lear, was the beginning of the corporate-owned jet. It was his belief that the traveling businessman needed a form of transportation to suit a hectic schedule. Today many corporations are buying small business jets almost as fast as they're being produced. Some companies may buy two or three jets at a time to meet the travel needs of their top-echelon executives.

This paragraph obviously has something to do with corporate jets. But what, exactly, is the writer trying to tell us about them? In the first sentence, we learn that the industry is growing at a fast rate. But there is little time to dwell on this idea because the second sentence quickly introduces a *new* thought: Bill Lear. Two sentences later we're told that many corporations are buying small business jets "almost as fast as they're being produced," but this statement doesn't tell us much of anything since we don't know how many corporations are buying the jets and how fast the jets are being produced.

What this paragraph lacks is a central theme—what the writer wants to tell us about corporate jets.

What this paragraph lacks is what I call an "umbrella thought."

Simply put, an umbrella thought is nothing more than the core idea of what you're trying to tell your reader at any given time. It's pretty much the same concept you learned in grammar school when a teacher talked about a "topic sentence" or in college composition, when the idea was embodied in something called the "thesis statement." I like "umbrella thought" because it's visual and concrete. You "open up" an umbrella thought so that it "covers" information within its scope.

Every well constructed paragraph should be covered by one umbrella thought, but the thought doesn't have to be expressed directly in any one sentence in the paragraph. Often your umbrella thought will be implied by the collective point of the information within the paragraph. Look at the following paragraph:

> The first thing we did that morning was visit the Museum of Modern Art. We spent about an hour there and later walked around Rockefeller Center for another hour. By then it was close to noon and so we went back to the hotel and had lunch.

The umbrella thought in this sentence is nothing more complicated than *what we did that morning*. Had the writer wanted to, he could have preceded the first sentence with, "Here's how we spent the morning," in which case we would have had an umbrella *statement*—that is, a statement reflecting the umbrella thought.

Enough definitions. Let's look now at a few examples of well-constructed paragraphs that illustrate the umbrella-thought concept.

From a *New Republic* editorial.

> It is an unusual court. It hasn't had a new member in five years. Like the Soviet's Politburo, it is a gerontocracy. The nine members average just under 68 years. Five are septuagenarians. Only two of the nine were named by Democratic presidents: Thurgood Marshall by Lyndon Johnson and Byron White by Kennedy. Nixon named four: the chief justice and Blackmun, Powell and Rehnquist. Eisenhower

picked two: Brennan and Potter Stewart; and Ford picked Stevens. Normally a president names a few justices in a four-year term, but no vacancy occurred during Carter's Presidency.

The umbrella thought in this paragraph is expressed in the first sentence. Notice how every sentence in this paragraph falls within the scope of the umbrella thought. You can precede most of the sentences with the phrase "The court is unusual because."

Here's another paragraph, from the opening of a Nora Ephron essay entitled "The Girls in the Office":

> I have not looked at *The Best of Everything* since I first bought it—in paperback—ten years ago, but I have a perverse fondness for it. In case you somehow missed it, *The Best of Everything* was a novel by Rona Jaffe about the lives of four, or was it five, single women in New York; it was pretty good trash, as trash goes, which is not why I am fond of it. I liked it because it seemed to me that it caught perfectly the awful essence of being a single woman in a big city. False pregnancies. Real pregnancies. Abortions. Cads. Dark bars with married men. Rampant masochism. I remember particularly a sequence in the book where one of the girls, rejected by a lover, goes completely bonkers and begins spending all her time spying on him, poking through his garbage for discarded love letters and old potato peelings; ultimately, as I recall, she falls from his fire escape to her death. The story seemed to me only barely exaggerated from what I was seeing around me, and, I am sorry to say, doing myself.

The paragraph concerns *The Best of Everything*. But the umbrella thought is *why Ms. Ephron has a perverse fondness for the book*. The thought isn't stated directly, as in the previous paragraph, but all the information in this paragraph falls *within* the thought; it tells the reader, in one way or another, why Ms. Ephron has a perverse fondness for this book.

Now a paragraph from John McPhee's essay about Bill Bradley, entitled "A Sense of Where You Are." The umbrella thought, very simply, is how Bill Bradley passes the ball.

> He passes as generously and as deftly as any player in the game. When he is dribbling, he can pass accurately without first catching the ball. He can also manage almost any pass without appearing to cock his arm or even bring his hand back. He just seems to flick his fingers and the ball is gone. Other Princeton players aren't always quite expecting Bradley's passes when they arrive, for Bradley is usually thinking a little bit ahead of everyone else on the floor. When he was a freshman, he was forever hitting his teammates on the mouth, the temple, or the back of the head with passes as accurate as they were surprising. His teammates have since sharpened their own faculties, and these accidents seldom happen now. "It's rewarding to play with him," one of them says. "If you get open, you'll get the ball." And, with all the defenders in between, it sometimes seems as if the ball has passed like a ray through several walls.

Reread this paragraph, but this time, before each sentence, think to yourself, "how Bradley passes the ball," and then take note of how each sentence simply presents another variation on the same theme.

One more example, from "The Medusa and the Snail," one of Lewis Thomas's essays. Here the umbrella thought is that we humans are not as unique as we think we are. Notice how in almost every sentence the same idea is presented, albeit in a different form.

> We tend to think of ourselves as the only wholly unique creations in nature, but it is not so. Uniqueness is so commonplace a property of living things that there is really nothing at all unique about it. A phenomenon can't be

unique and universal at the same time. Even individual free-swimming bacteria can be viewed as unique entities, distinguishable from each other even when they are the progeny of a single clone. Spudich and Koshland have recently reported that motile microorganisms of the same species are like solitary eccentrics in their swimming behavior. When they are searching for food, some tumble in one direction for precisely so many seconds before quitting, while others tumble differently and for different, but characteristic, periods of time. If you watch them closely, tethered by their flagellae to the surface of an antibody-coated slide, you can tell them from each other by the way they twirl, as accurately as though they had different names.

I often refer to this practice of repeating words or phrases that either repeat or reinforce the idea embodied in the umbrella thought as "anchoring," the idea being to keep important thoughts vivid in your reader's mind. Most writing instructors endorse the basic principle of "anchoring," but some warn that when you repeat words or even patterns of word order, you run the risk of boring the reader, and so they advise you to vary the presentation with synonyms or with syntax that contrasts the patterns you've already established. I'm certainly not "anti-variety" in my basic approach to writing, but I've found that most of my students have an easier time producing paragraphs that reflect variety than they do producing paragraphs that read clearly and cohesively. Sometimes when I'm reading a paragraph in which a student is making an obvious attempt *not* to repeat a word or phrase, I can visualize the student foraging through a thesaurus for synonyms. I'm not sure where you draw the line between repetition that reinforces communication and repetition that diminishes it, but the priorities here, I think are clear: you strive for clarity *first;* then you concern yourself with variety.

Putting the Concept to Work

Now that you have a grasp of the umbrella-thought concept, let's put it to work. Here's a paragraph from *Vogue* magazine that presents a series of facts but no umbrella thought.

> In the late 1960s and throughout most of the '70s, stores sought out name designers as keys to exclusivity. In 1968, Bonwit Teller was the first store in New York to carry Calvin Klein clothes. Similarly, at one time, Bloomingdale's was the only store in the country with a Perry Ellis shop. Today Calvin's and Perry's clothes are each sold at about three hundred stores across the country. With the proliferation of designer labels it has become increasingly difficult for any one store to distinguish itself from others.

The writer here wants to get across the fact that designer clothing, once a key to exclusivity in many stores, has become so commonplace that stores can no longer use the labels as a reflection of their uniqueness. Here's a revision that incorporates the umbrella-thought concept.

> For a while there, from the late 1960s to the late 1970s, you could tell one department store from another by the designer-label clothes it carried. If you wanted to dress yourself in Calvin Klein in 1968, for instance, there was only one store you could shop—Bonwit Teller. And if you were interested in Perry Ellis, Bloomingdale's was the only store in the country you could go to. No more. Calvin's and Perry's clothes are available today in some three hundred different stores throughout the country, and the proliferation of designer labels has become so pronounced over the past few years that it is becoming increasingly difficult for any department store to distinguish itself from its competition.

In the first sentence, we introduce the umbrella thought, guiding reader's focus to how, in the past, you could tell one department store from another. The next two sentences maintain the same focus, but this time with more specific examples. "No more," in the third sentence, tells the reader we're changing focus. But with "Calvin's and Perry's" leading off the next and final sentence, we stay within the umbrella thought and use the previous focal points to introduce new material.

I urge you not to take the umbrella-thought concept for granted—to dismiss it as perhaps too "elementary" a consideration to worry about when you write. Try it. Get into the habit, *before* you start a paragraph, of writing down the umbrella thought, and keep the thought in view (as well as in mind) *as* you're developing the idea. You'll be surprised at how much the technique will help to improve the cohesiveness of your paragraphs, and their impact.

Big Thoughts and Little Thoughts

A basic axiom of effective writing is that there should be consistency between the way you present your material and the priorities that underlie the presentation. This means, in short, that if an idea or an image is important, you should treat it as such—give the idea its due. Look at the following sentence:

> An invalid since the age of three, Bartlett was born in Columbus, Ohio.

The way this sentence is constructed, with "An invalid since the age of three" as a subordinate introductory phrase and "Bartlett was born in Columbus, Ohio" as the main clause, what the writer is "saying" to the reader is this: Bartlett's being born in Columbus, Ohio, is the more important of the two thoughts. If this is what the writer had in mind, well and good. But if the writer had wanted Bartlett's invalid state to occupy most of the spotlight, he should have written the sentence as follows:

> Born in Columbus, Ohio, Bartlett has been an invalid since the age of three.

Here's a similar example:

> As Charlie watches the two or three movies he makes it a point to see every Friday night, he always has a box of buttered popcorn in his lap.

As written, the important thought here is the fact that Charlie keeps a box of buttered popcorn in his lap. But if the writer had wanted to emphasize Charlie's movie-going habits, using the popcorn as a supporting detail, he would have been better off with something like this:

> Charlie enjoys movies so much that every Friday night he makes it a point to see two or three of them, a box of buttered popcorn constantly in his lap.

The principle at work here, as I've already mentioned, is a very simple one: *give to important thoughts the kind of presentation they deserve*. To help you make use of this principle in your writing, I recommend a technique I often suggest to my students. The technique consists merely of assigning to those thoughts you consider important with respect to your umbrella thought a designation that recognizes this importance. Let's call them "big thoughts." And once you've decided that a thought warrants this designation, you give it special treatment. Here are some guidelines to govern how you treat big thoughts.

1. Never (well, almost never) express a big thought as a subordinate phrase or clause.

2. Try to limit the number of big thoughts in each sentence to no more than two, and when you're using more

than one, make sure each thought is expressed in an independent clause.

3. When you're using "little thoughts"—ideas or images that reinforce a big thought—express the big thought first and follow it with the supporting little thoughts.

Spacing Out Your Big Thoughts

Good nonfiction writing is often characterized by a quality I like to describe as breathing space. You rarely get the feeling of being crowded when you read it, because the writers give you plenty of breathing space. The ideas and images are comfortably spaced instead of being crammed into overloaded sentences. Here's an example of the kind of writing I'm talking about from an essay by Richard Lemon that appeared in the "My Turn" section of *Newsweek*.

> Like Reagan, I love jelly beans. Like him, I kept a jar of them on my desk during my last job, which involved lots of visitors. Like him, I observed the way people went about picking their jelly beans (licorice, I think he will agree, is the most controversial), although I was never judgmental about it and I've learned things that suggest he is. I quit that job twenty months ago to write on my own, and since the huge pitcher of jelly beans I was given as a farewell present has been gone, I haven't eaten any. The reason I haven't is that the jelly bean is essentially gregarious. It comes in many friendly colors, it is hospitable, and it has something for everyone except bluenoses from Onondaga.

The sentences in this paragraph vary in length. Some of them are fairly lengthy, a few running as long as forty words. What's more, about half the sentences have dependent clauses, such as "which involved lots of visitors" in the second sentence. What's important, though, is that Lemon gives his big thought plenty of breathing space. The main ideas (i.e., big thoughts) are expressed in independent clauses. Compare the following sentence in which I deliberately jam thoughts together to the original that follows.

I quit that job twenty months ago to write on my own, and since the huge pitcher of jelly beans I was given as a farewell present has been gone, I haven't eaten any.

When I quit that job twenty months ago to write on my own, I received, as a farewell present, a huge pitcher of jelly beans that is now gone, even though I haven't eaten any.

Here's another paragraph in which comfortably spaced big thoughts make for a comfortable reading experience. This is the opening of an essay in *Esquire* that James Wolcott wrote about author Studs Terkel.

Studs Terkel has become America's favorite barroom philosopher. When he turns up on radio and television talk shows to trot out a few treasured anecdotes, you can almost hear the clatter of glasses and laughter in the background, the *brr ping!* of a distant pinball machine. Terkel has built an impressive career on informal chat; he hosts a weekday radio show in Chicago that is broadcast nationally, and he is the author of five volumes of oral reminiscences, the most recent *American Dreams: Lost and Found*. In the flesh, Terkel is affable foxy-eyed, unpretentious; you can't help liking the sly old spitballer. And his books—particularly his volume on the depression, *Hard Times*—all have their spurts of humor, insight and poignancy.

Again, let's take a slice of this paragraph and suggest what Wolcott *could* have done had he not been as careful about spacing out his thoughts:

Terkel's impressive career, based on informal chat, is built around a nationally broadcast, Chicago-based radio program, and around the five books of oral reminiscences he has written, the most recent *American Dreams: Lost and Found.*

Note that even though we've compressed some of the ideas in this passage—instead of "he hosts a weekday radio show in Chicago that is broadcast nationally," we say, "his nationally broadcast, Chicago-based radio program"—the change doesn't enhance the readability of the passage. Thus we see that conciseness, something you generally *strive* for in writing, doesn't always produce clarity—not if the changes rob important thoughts of the space they need to register on the reader with clarity and impact. It's one thing to reduce the number of words you use to express a thought and something else again to reduce the number of words it takes to express a thought in the most effective manner. The point is to base your decisions on thoughts, not on words.

I can't emphasize enough the importance of this distinction between thoughts and words. It isn't the number of words in a sentence that determines how easy or how difficult a time your reader will have absorbing the information in that sentence; rather, it's the number of thoughts your reader's mind has to process within the time it takes to read the sentence. And more than simply the *number* of thoughts, the nature and difficulty of these thoughts. Take a look at the following two sentences from an essay by anthropologist and naturalist Loren Eiseley, "The Great Deeps."

They have seen it [a sea-born protoplasm] in the delicate "snowshoe" feet of desert lizards devised for running over sand. From some unknown spot, most probably along the shoals above the continental shelf, it has reached out into lakes and grasslands, edged stealthily into deserts, learned even to endure the heat of boiling springs or to hatch eggs, like the emperor penquin, in the blizzards by the southern pole.

Eiseley's second sentence, which runs nearly fifty words, is three times as long as the first, but is nonetheless the clearer of the two. This is because there is really only one *big* thought in this sentence—where the "it" has spread to. But in the previous sentence, there are two thoughts: (1) the fact that men have seen the protoplasm in the delicate "snowshoe" feet of desert lizards; and (2) the fact that these special feet enable the lizard to move quickly across sand. For more clarity, Eiseley might have spaced these two thoughts as follows:

> They have seen it in the delicate "snowshoe" feet of desert lizards—those feet, by the way, so ingeniously devised for running over sand.

What have we done here? Nothing more complicated than to draw a clear distinction between the two thoughts: the big thought—the fact that the protoplasm can be seen in the "snowshoe" feet of desert lizards; and the smaller, less important thought—what those feet enable the lizard to do.

Priming: How to Make Your Reader More Receptive

By this time, it shouldn't be necessary for me to dwell upon the difference between meaning and impact: you already know. But what you may not know is that while the meaning of a thought is pretty much a fixed property, the impact of a thought can vary considerably, depending on any number of factors.

Look at the following two sentences:

Reducing government spending is the only way we're ever going to curb inflation.

There's only one way to curb inflation: we have to reduce government spending.

Each of these sentences expresses the same thought. Each is written clearly. Yet the second sentence has more impact. The reason: we've taken measures to enhance the impact of the thought. We've used the first part of the sentence—"There's only one way to curb inflation"—to make the reader more receptive to the thought. In other words, we've primed the reader to receive the information that we want to get across to him with impact.

Here are two other examples that illustrate the same concept:

A recent General Accounting Office report, in which a dozen parks were surveyed, estimated that improvements to the entire system would cost $1.6 billion and would put enormous strain on a system that this year will have to make do on a $497 million budget that has not kept up with inflation.

A recent General Accounting Office report details just how serious the problems are. The GAO surveyed a dozen parks and estimated that improvements to the entire system would cost $1.6 billion. This is an enormous strain for a system that this year will have to make do on a $497 million budget that has not kept up with inflation.

Here again we have two passages conveying essentially the same information, neither of them suffering from any obvious grammatical problems. But, again, the second example has noticeably more clarity, and for the same reason as in the previous second version. Instead of obliging the reader to absorb several pieces of information in one big gulp, this second version feeds information to the reader in easily digestible portions. More than that, it feeds the information in logical *stages*. The phrase "just how serious the problems are" presents a general idea that makes the reader more receptive to the statistics that follow.

The technique at work here is easier to explain than to execute. Essentially, it's a matter of breaking up a complicated thought—i.e., a thought that your reader might have some difficulty in processing—into a general statement followed by specific details. Let's illustrate the technique again. Here's a first version:

> There was almost no credible explanation for this until, in 1978, a University of California team discovered that when a group of volunteers who had just had their wisdom teeth extracted were divided into two groups, with one group given morphine as a painkiller and the other group given a placebo, a third of the placebo patients reported a dramatic reduction in pain.

And here's the revision:

> There was almost no credible explanation for this until, in 1978, a University of California team made a startling discovery. In a group of volunteers who had just had their wisdom teeth extracted, some received morphine as a painkiller, others were given a placebo. A third of the placebo patients reported a dramatic reduction in pain.

The staging statement in the revision is "made a startling discovery." Why? Because it helps "set the stage" for the information that follows.

Here's another example. In the first passage, I'll show you how Nora Ephron *might* have presented her ideas if she hadn't chosen to stage them. The second passage shows how she actually wrote the passage in an essay called "Divorce, Maryland Style."

Within a few weeks of the governor's walkout, Mrs. Mandel realized that the friends she had counted on to side with her sided instead with the governor and his power.

Within a few weeks of the governor's walkout, Mrs. Mandel realized she had made a terrible mistake. She had counted on her friends to side with her—and they sided with the governor and his power.

The difference between these two passages isn't monumental, but the second has more impact. Why? Because the staging phrase, "made a terrible mistake," sets us up for the information that follows.

Priming, then, is nothing more than saying to your reader, in effect, "Get ready, I have some information that might interest you." Priming is what you do when you have exciting news to share with a friend and you start out by saying, "I have the most exciting news to tell you. Sit down and listen." Staging is Mark Antony bellowing, "Friends, Romans, countrymen, lend me your ears." Priming is a Las Vegas emcee stretching out his introduction of the show, the better to trigger a big ovation. ("And now, ladies and gentlemen, the moment I'm sure you've all been waiting for. Direct from New York, and making his debut at the fabulous Sands . . .") Priming is the step you take to make sure your reader is going to pay attention to what you want him to absorb. Priming, in short, is what Michael Korda does in this passage from *Success!*, which we'll examine sentence by sentence.

The conventional view is that the demands of achievement lead to ulcers, hypertension, heart attacks, impotence and early death. We constantly hear of people who have "worked themselves to death." But anybody familiar with life at the top soon observes that a remarkably large percentage of high achievers are fit, healthy and active.

Statistics bear this out. A study by the Metropolitan Life

Insurance Company reveals that successful executives as a group enjoy longer life and better health than the average American. Their mortality rate is only 63 percent of that of the total white, adult, male population. The presidents of *Fortune*'s top five hundred corporations did even better. Their rate was only 5 percent of the average mortality, indicating that big time success is not only rewarded with money, but also with longevity and good health.

The big thought Korda wants to drive home here is this: successful executives, contrary to popular opinion, are not only very rich but rather healthy as well. Let's look at how his staging of the material drives this point home with clarity and impact.

> The conventional view is that the demands of achievement lead to ulcers, hypertension, heart attacks, impotence and early death. We constantly hear of people who have "worked themselves to death." But anybody familiar with life at the top soon observes that a remarkably large percentage of high achievers are fit, healthy and active.

Korda introduces the point he is about to disprove. Note how smoothly he shifts focus. "The conventional view" feeds naturally into "We constantly hear"; then he introduces the rebuttal with "But." Let's go on.

> Statistics bear this out.

Here is what amounts to an appetizer. Not the statistics themselves, but a statement that says, "Get ready for some numbers." A staging statement.

> A study by the Metropolitan Life Insurance Company reveals that successful executives as a group enjoy longer life and better health than the average American.

What's this? Yes, another staging statement. Instead of going directly to the numbers after "reveals that," Korda takes his time.

> Their mortality rate is only 63 percent of that of the total white, adult, male population.

A single statistic, for which we've been well prepared. And Korda gives it its own stage.

> The presidents of *Fortune*'s top five hundred corporations did even better.

Still another staging statement. It breaks up the presentation of numbers. "Did even better" tells us what the numbers are going to say before we receive them.

> Their rate was only 5 percent of the average mortality, indicating that big time success is not only rewarded with money, but also with longevity and good health.

Keep in mind here that it's the *staging* of the material that makes these two paragraphs work. Korda gives us a general picture, priming us for more specific data. He holds on to our focus while deftly parceling out bits of information that not only take us somewhere but keep us interested along the way.

Reinforcing Big Thoughts

It isn't only what you give your reader *prior* to an important thought that can enhance the impact of that thought, it's what you give him immediately *after* you introduce the thought—which brings up a concept I like to call "big-thought reinforcement."

It's a simple concept and I can hardly lay claim to authorship. It's nothing more complicated than making sure you reinforce general thoughts with supporting details that are meaningful and concrete. And the bigger the thought, the more details you need. Look at the following sentence which begins a paragraph in Peter Ross Range's *Playboy* piece, "The Technology War: Behind Japanese Lines."

> Japan is the most pervasively prosperous country on earth.

That's a big statement, and it's clearly written. But unless Range backs up that statement with details that reinforce it, it will have little impact. So here is what Range does.

> Japan is the most pervasively prosperous country on earth. Everybody has a nice stereo, everybody has a telephone and everybody has a color-TV set that not only flashes balls, strikes and outs during every pitch of every baseball game but also computes the speed of each pitch, in kilometers, by the time the ball hits the catcher's mitt—as well as the batter's current batting average after every time at bat. Japan is the country with over 99 percent literacy and three national newspapers selling a total of 25,000,000 copies per day. It is the country with the highest life expectancy—78 for women, 73 for men—of any nation in the world except Iceland. It is the country where trains run so perfectly on time that if you board the 12:10 for Kyoto at 12:10 and 30 seconds, you are getting onto another train using that same platform to head for someplace else. It is the country where the taxi drivers still open and shut the door for you—without getting out of their seats (it is done mechanically via a lever attached to the steering column).

I could go on. There are another two or three paragraphs whose details do what the details in this paragraph do: pay off the main idea; that Japan is the "most pervasively prosperous country on earth." Range doesn't ask his readers to take *his* word for it; he supplies the data that makes the statement evident to anybody.

You would be hard-pressed to find any successful nonfiction writer for whom the need to reinforce general statements with supporting details isn't instinctive. Good writers know that it isn't so much the *words* you use that create impact—it's the ideas and images that the words convey. Look at how writer Arthur Zich introduces, in a *Signature* article, the idea that garlic consumption is on the rise, and the lengths to which he goes to reinforce the point.

> In the past decade alone, garlic consumption in the U.S. has doubled. Gilroy can't meet the need; imports from Mexico, Spain and South America are on the rise. And the end is not in sight. Nowadays, no restaurateur with even the vaguest gourmet pretensions would dream of fielding a menu without garlic bread, escargots with garlic butter or Caesar salad. No cuisine-conscious kitchen captain—housewife or househusband—could do without a handy kitchen garlic press. No Westport, Conn., or Mill Valley, Calif., grocer would be caught without shelves full of garlic sausages, garlic cheese dips, garlic salad dressings, garlic salt, flakes, powder and paste, not to mention imported French aioli—garlic mayonnaise.

Is there any doubt in your mind that garlic consumption in on the rise?

And look how John McPhee gives us detail after detail to back up the general statement he makes at the beginning of this paragraph, from his essay "The Headmaster."

> Boyden's principle of athletics for all has remained one of the main elements of the school's program, and Deerfield is unmatched in this respect today. Where once he did not have enough boys for even one team, he now has teams for all five hundred. When a boy at Deerfield chooses a sport, he automatically makes a team that has a full schedule of games with other schools. For example, Deerfield usually has at least eight basketball teams, each with game uniforms, away games, and all the other incidentals of the sport on the varsity level. This is true in soccer, baseball, football, tennis, lacrosse, hockey, squash, swimming, skiing, track,

and cross-country as well. With few exceptions, everybody in Deerfield is required to take part in three sports a year. There is no set number of teams in any sport. According to the boys' choices, there may be a few more football teams one year and a few more soccer teams the next. Deerfield has sent on a share of athletic stars—football players such as Mutt Ray to Dartmouth and Archie Roberts to Columbia, for instance—but Deerfield is not really an atmosphere in which a great athlete is likely to develop. The headmaster's belief in sport is exceeded by his belief that everything has its place and time. Deerfield athletes are given no time for extra practice, nor are they permitted to practice any sport out of season. In the fall and the spring, the basketball courts are locked and baskets are actually removed from the backboards.

Granted, because he writes for *The New Yorker,* a magazine that sets few limits on the length of the pieces it runs, McPhee can go into deeper detail than writers who contribute to other publications. Still, it's worth noting the sheer *number* of details McPhee feels obliged to present to support the general idea he is trying to get across. Indeed, we see in this abundance of reinforcing details one of the chief differences between accomplished writers like McPhee and less accomplished writers, in particular student writers. Writers who have yet to master their craft tend to build their pieces with an abundance of general ideas backed up by relatively little in the way of reinforcing details. In accomplished writers, by contrast, you find a noticeably greater ratio of reinforcing details to general points, as we see in the following two passages: one from a piece in *New West* by Mard Naman, the other, a William Zinsser essay called "But is it Literature?"

The first time I visited the New Age Dentist's office I thought I had accidentally walked into a singles bar. There were ferns everywhere. Redwood ceiling beams. Redwoodframed mirrors. Beautiful dental assistants. Sincere eye contact. Taped music by Gato Barbieri and Linda Ronstadt. A dentist (no white smock) who Explains What He's Doing. Who is not just a technician—no!—but the host for an oral experience.

Therefore he wants Bruce Catton to tell him everything that happened in the Civil War, and why, and he wants Samuel Eliot Morison to tell him what happened to America in the years before and since. He wants Barbara Tuchman to tell him how the guns of August happened to start World War I, and William L. Shirer to trace the rise of the Third Reich that started an even bigger war. He wants to learn anatomy of Britain and the meaning of treason. He wants Alan Moorehead to take him down the Nile, Thor Heyerdahl to take him across the Pacific, Theodore H. White to take him along on the making and unmaking of Presidents, Arthur Schlesinger, Jr., to take him over the new frontier's thousand days. He wants James Baldwin and Sammy Davis to lead him back through their tormented boyhoods so that he can discover his past sins and try to absolve them.

In the Naman example above, there are seven supporting details for the main general idea—the similarity between the New Age Dentist's office and a singles bar. In the Zinsser example, there are more than a dozen reinforcing details to back up the idea of what a modern reader wants from his books. Both Naman and Zinsser understand—as John McPhee does—that the impact of a general point is not determined so much by how it's phrased as by the number and quality of the ideas and images that *reinforce* that point. Learn from their example.

Orchestrating Your Reinforcing Details

One of the things you're forced to do almost constantly when you're writing certain types of expository pieces is to decide which reinforcing ideas and images do the most effective job of backing up your general points. And making such decisions is complicated by the fact that ideas and images capable of reinforcing an idea can take a number of forms.

Let's assume, for the moment, that you're writing an article about a corporation that enjoys an unusually high level of productivity. Among the *kinds* of reinforcing details you might use to stage the information in such a piece are the following:

1. Statistics comparing the performances of the corporation and its competitors.
2. Statements from corporation employees.
3. Statements from corporation supervisors.
4. A general account of everyday occurrences that illustrate productivity.
5. *Specific* incidents that illustrate productivity.

Depending on any number of factors—among them, the length of the piece you're writing and the kind of information you have at your disposal—your use of these details will vary. However, there is a certain pattern that shows up time and again in well-written articles. It is a general-to-specific pattern typified in the following paragraph from a Harry Stein piece on softball that appeared in *Esquire*.

> According to statistics of the Oklahoma City-based Amateur Softball Association, there are some 110,000 teams of serious softball players in the country today, up from 29,000 just a decade ago. In New York's Rockland County (the area about twenty miles northwest of New York City, where

Bandy plays most of his ball) there are no fewer than forty softball leagues, each consisting of at least ten teams, most with a roster of twenty men. Nor are the players confined to a single economic stratum. There are bartenders, and businessmen, salesmen and school teachers. One fellow, a pitcher for a team in Paterson, New Jersey, gave up a $65,000-a-year job as a stockbroker to drive a cab because the Wall Street routine hadn't allowed him to play more than a couple of days a week. Another guy—now in his late thirties, a legendary figure in Rockland County softball circles—sacrificed not only a good job at a bank but also his marriage of fourteen years and his three children; he currently lives on his savings in southern California and plays softball full time.

Look at where this paragraph began—*all* the people who play softball. And look at where it ended: on one specific player. This is a classic illustration of a pattern I call "narrowing down." You start with a general thought and gradually narrow down to more specific details. Here's another paragraph that illustrates the same pattern, this from a *Signature* piece on sneakers by Jeff Greenfield.

The boom has revolutionized footwear. For years, quality shoe stores refused to stock sneakers, sending customers to sporting good stores instead. Now, with the American footwear industry down two years in a row—for the first time since World War II—sneaker sales are growing by 15 to 25 percent a year. They account for more than half the total sales of many of the biggest sporting goods stores. Whole new retail enterprises have sprung up, selling nothing but athletic and casual footwear, places with names like Sneaker World, Athlete's Foot and Sneaker Circus.

Here again, we start with general information and eventually focus down to something highly specific—actual stores.

I mention this general-to-specific pattern to serve as a

guideline, not a straitjacket. You can vary the pattern in any number of ways, depending on the kind of material you're using to back up your main points. What's more, we're talking here about only one kind of writing situation: an expository paragraph in which you're trying to get across a big point with supporting details.

But the pattern, all the same, is useful to bear in mind.

Some Final Thoughts on Staging

It would be nice to be able to spell out some specific rules that might bring into clearer focus for you the techniques of staging I've been talking about throughout this chapter. But staging techniques should always be keyed to the material you're presenting, which means it's all but impossible to come up with hard and fast principles. In any event, here are a few general observations on how to become more skilled in the art of staging.

The first step, as I have noted several times throughout this chapter, is to concentrate your attention on the thoughts you're trying to express rather than on the words you're using to express these thoughts. Keep in mind the general principles relating to these thoughts—the value, for instance, of spacing out your big thoughts.

As to becoming more adept at using the staging techniques themselves, a good way to begin is to look for staging devices in the magazine or newspaper articles you read. The weekly news magazines—*Time* and *Newsweek,* in particular—use such devices all the time. And anytime you're writing, *think* staging. Don't simply present an armful of data to your reader. Break the information down. Get into the habit of telling your reader *ahead of time* what you're going to tell him, in more detail, a little later. And when you're going over something you've read and sense that you're piling on too much information at one time, use the staging techniques we've talked about in this chapter. There is nothing technically complicated about staging: it's mainly a matter of sensing when it's necessary and going ahead and doing it. Do it enough and it will eventually become a natural element of your writing style.

5

A New Look
at Description

DESCRIPTION poses a nettlesome problem to a reader-oriented writer. For no matter how vividly you write descriptive passages, the average nonfiction reader today has only limited tolerance for it. Description, remember, doesn't tell a story and doesn't usually provide practical information. Consequently, many readers can get along very nicely without it, thank you. Glossing over lengthy descriptive passages is one of the first things they teach you in speed-writing courses.

So what's a writer to do? Simply forget about descriptive writing? Dismiss it as a superfluous and outdated skill, like being able to drop-kick a football forty yards? Not quite. Description still has an important place in contemporary nonfiction and especially in certain types of feature writing. It's as important as ever to be able to create in the mind of your reader vivid impressions of the people, places, things, and scenes you're writing about. But it's also important today that you tailor your descriptive writing to the changing appetite of the average reader. Above all, you have to exercise economy and restraint when you're writing description: you have to be able to create in only two or three sentences images that a generation or two ago you might have been able to express in two or three paragraphs. And you have to be wary of feeding your reader too much *pure* description at one time. Wherever possible and practical, you need to integrate descriptive material into your narrative, weave it in and out of your expository information. In other words, you have to be able to accomplish what writers have always had to accomplish with description, but you have to do so in fewer words and in a form your readers will find appealing. In this chapter, we'll look at a few of the techniques designed to help your description do the job it is supposed to do, and do it well.

Looking at the Basics

There is essentially only one objective when you write description: to create pictures in the mind of your reader. But there are two kinds of details you can use to create these pictures: (1) purely factual details—details that describe persons, objects, places, or scenes objectively and concretely; or, (2) what might be called impressionistic details: details that produce in the reader's mind a general sense of the picture you're trying to create, leaving it up to the reader to develop his own more specific images.

Here are two examples of description built upon *factual* details:

> Charlie Foster is forty-two years old, is six feet tall, and weighs 175 pounds. His hair is gray and curly. His eyes are dark brown.

> The living room was furnished with eighteenth-century French antiques. Along the far wall was a floor-to-ceiling bookcase, most of whose shelves were stacked with old books. Beside the bookcase was a picture window that overlooked a small pond.

In each of the above passages, the writer is acting as a recorder of objective details. The details speak for themselves.

Here are descriptions of the same objects written in a purely impressionistic vein.

Charlie Foster is in his early forties and still looks as if he could fill in at shortstop for most big-league teams. His hair has a Little Orphan Annie look to it, and it's obvious that he doesn't dye it. He has sexy eyes.

The living room looked like a salon you might find in Paris. Along the far wall was a bookcase straight out of an eighteenth-century novel. Beside the bookcase was a picture window that revealed a scene that wouldn't have been out of place in a Cézanne painting.

Clearly, we're taking more for granted with these two passages. We're assuming, for instance, that the reader would know how a big-league shortstop is built and would be able to picture a salon in Paris or a Cézanne landscape. That's a big assumption—maybe too big.

Now look at the following passages, in which we *combine* the two types of detail.

Charlie Foster is forty-two years old, a trim six-footer who looks as if he could still fill in at shortstop for most big-league teams. His gray hair is curly—he looks like a male Orphan Annie—and his brown eyes give off what some people still call a "bedroom look."

The living room was furnished with eighteenth-century French antiques and looked like a salon you might find in Paris. Along the far wall was a floor-to-ceiling bookcase, most of whose shelves were stacked with old books—the kind of books you might expect to find in a museum. Beside the bookcase was a picture window which overlooked a small pond, a soft pastoral scene that would not have seemed out of place in a Cézanne painting.

These last two examples create pictures more vivid than those created in the previous descriptions. The reason, simply, is that the two kinds of details—the factual and impressionistic—reinforce one another when you combine them. And this is the technique, the *combination* of factual and impressionistic details, that we're going to be discussing in this chapter.

How to Describe People

As briefly as possible, please. For although most feature writing obliges you to describe the people you're writing about, you rarely have more than a couple of sentences to do the job. This constraint wouldn't be as troublesome were it not for the fact that people differ from each other in so many ways: height, weight, age, build, complexion, facial features, hair—not to mention dress, or speech, or comportment, or the general psychological impression people convey when you meet them: whether they're friendly or shy or hostile.

Let's not get carried away. It's obvious that you can't cram everything describable about a person into a two- or even three-sentence description. You have to choose and zero in on those few characteristics that most vividly convey the essence of the people you're describing. At the same time, you need to present this description in a brief, capsulized form. Let's look now at the technique the top pros use when confronted with the same problem.

The Main Pattern: General Impression to Specific Detail

I find it useful in my writing class to teach descriptive writing in terms of the patterns used by the better nonfiction writers. One such pattern, extensively used, starts the reader off with an impressionistic detail (in many cases an adjective hooked to the word "looking," as in "athletic-look-ing, "prosperous-looking," etc.) and quickly reinforces this image with two or three factual details. Here are some ex-amples:

> Phil Evans is a prosperous-looking man who keeps his salt-and-pepper hair short and favors dark, conservatively tai-lored suits.

> Miriam in an athletic-looking woman: trim and short-haired and brisk in her movements.

> Chambers is a robust-looking man in his late forties, with a wide face, a ruddy complexion, a full head of white hair, and an easy smile.

There are any number of adjectives you can link with the word "looking" when you employ this pattern, but be care-ful. To describe a person as "fat-looking" or "tall-looking," for instance, makes no sense. Keep in mind, too, that this pattern has impact only when the impressionistic phrase is followed by two or three factual details that back it up.

Variations on the Basic Pattern

Starting off your capsule descriptions of people with an impressionistic detail and then buttressing it by factual details is by no means the only pattern you can use. Some writers like to *reverse* this pattern—that is, start out with several factual details and close out the description with an impressionistic detail. Here's Helen Lawrenson using this technique to describe two people in a piece she wrote for *Esquire:*

Boo Brassey, English, with short, straight, black hair and bangs, narrow black eyes, and an odd catlike face . . . Bootsie, a girl with long, fair hair and a school girl look.

Another variation is to begin with a series of factual details to introduce your main impressionistic detail and then reinforce the impressionistic detail with more factual details. Here's an illustration from Truman Capote's *In Cold Blood:*

> Though he wore rimless glasses and was of but average height, standing just under five feet ten, Mr. Clutter cut a man's-man figure. His shoulders were broad, his hair had held its dark color, his square-jawed confident face retained a healthy-hued youthfulness, and his teeth, unstained and strong enough to shatter walnuts, were still intact.

The initial details in the first sentence are *factual:* "wore rimless glasses," "was of but average height, standing just under five feet ten." But these details are subordinate to the chief descriptive detail of the sentence: "Mr. Clutter cut a man's-man figure," which, you will notice, is immediately reinforced by the phrase "His shoulders were broad," a factual detail. Capote, by the way, blends factual and impressionistic details as smoothly as anybody. Let's look now at one of the more subtle techniques he uses to make this mix more effective.

The Abstract-Concrete Tandem

One of the phrases Capote used in the passage quoted, "square-jawed confident face," is worth noting because it represents a technique skilled writers use frequently—the juxtaposition of a factual detail—"square-jawed"—with a more abstract impressionistic detail—"confident"—in describing the same object.

Strictly speaking, of course, there is no such thing as a "confident" face. What Capote is really saying is that Clutter had a square-jawed face that gave the impression of confidence. Capote uses a descriptive shorthand here that can work well for you as long as you don't misuse or overuse the device. Here are some other examples of the device:

His child had alert, blue eyes.

Her uncle had a muscular, aggressive build.

She had a small, angry mouth.

Granted, we're taking liberties. There is no such thing, really, as "alert eyes," or an "aggressive build," or an "angry mouth." But the juxtaposition of abstract and concrete conveys the image more vividly and economically than a more literal rendering such as "blue eyes that gave the impression of alertness," or "a build that made him appear aggressive."

Be careful. Get sloppy with this shorthand construction and you can end up with absurd images: noses that are "intelligent," or hair that is "happy." Use this technique the way a master chef uses a strong, distinctive spice: precisely and judiciously.

Figurative Devices: Description, Express-Style

Among the most useful tools at your disposal when you're describing people are figurative devices: metaphors, similes, and the like. Look at the simile used by Aaron Latham to lead off an article he wrote for *Esquire* about Clark Clifford:

Clark Clifford's face looks as if it belonged on a hundred-dollar bill.

Or Gary Wills's description of former Nixon aide Dwight Chapin:

> Dwight Chapin looks like a young Bert Parks, with regular features and patent-leather hair.

And consider the following two passages, the first by George Plimpton describing the owner of a professional football team, the second by Helen Lawrenson describing producer Michael Butler. The Lawrenson description, by the way, could probably benefit from judicious editing: the sentence is too long and involved; but I like it for its content not its syntax.

> A slight thin figure, he was very nattily dressed in a dark pinstriped suit, making his way through the locker room somewhat nervously with an abstracted air, as if he had put an expensive pair of cuff links down and could not remember exactly where.

> That weekend was the first time I'd ever seen him and when he came into the room, tall, lean, elegant in a beautifully tailored olive green Nehru-style jacket and cream-colored riding breeches, his chestnut hair cut modishly long, his dark brown Zapata moustache (Eugenia Sheppard once wrote "the Racquet and Tennis Club does his moustache") and his large and faintly melancholy brown eyes all gave him the appearance of some dashing Hungarian prince in a forgotten Lehar operetta.

More than anything else, what's at work in the above passages is a writer's imagination: a writer's ability to reach into his own experience for a reference that imbues a description with added texture, resonance, and precision. But at the same time, there are technical devices through which the writer injects this imaginative input into the description. I can't tell you how to create your own similes and metaphors, but here is a brief list of the simple constructions that are almost invariably present when a writer is enriching his descriptions with figurative devices.

1. ... *as if* ...

Paul Reese always manages to look *as if* he just came back from a Caribbean vacation.

Melinda Phillips's face looks *as if* it belongs on a *Vogue* cover.

When Richard Gassett talks to you, he tends to lower his voice and lean forward *as if* he were revealing to you some dark secret.

2. ... *gives the appearance* ... ; ... *gives the impression* ... ; ... *looks like* ...

Paul Watson *looks like* a bank president. He is slim, grayhaired, distinguished-looking, and wears only dark blue suits.

Betty Ann is a thin, intense, dark-haired woman in her late thirties who always *gives* you *the impression* that she is running fifteen minutes late even when she's on time.

3. ... *has the* ——— *of* ...

Jerry Forbes has the cool, worldly look of a wealthy European businessman who never has to make more than one phone call to find a beautiful woman he can take to dinner.

Miriam Foster has the stern, bookish look of a librarian whose biggest secret is that she hates books.

"As if," "gives the impression," "looks like"—there are at least a dozen similar constructions, any one of which can express a personal observation in a description. Get into the habit of using them. Practice (yes, practice) using them. If you're sitting somewhere with time to kill—in a dentist's waiting room, in an airline terminal, on a train—look around and see if you can mentally fashion descriptions built around comparisons and analogies. Make a game of it. Look at a person and then try to complete the following sentence: "She looks like the kind of woman who would . . . ." You may be surprised at how clever and imaginative you can be when you train your thought in a certain direction.

Interweaving Description and Narrative

As I suggested at the beginning of this chapter, nonfiction readers are generally less receptive to *pure* description than they are to descriptive material mixed with other kinds of material. Here's a good example of this mix from a profile novelist Leonard Gardner wrote about boxer Roberto Durán in *Inside Sports*.

> Duran put his tape deck on the table, sprawled in a chair, and began loudly beating time on the table. He was bearded, wore a T-shirt in praise of Panama, jeans, a white cap and a pair of rainbow suspenders. His black eyes gazed vacantly, his head and shoulders rocked, and he appeared a captive of his own restless energy. He let out a few sharp cries, then took up a knife and spoon, beating them together even as the waitress took the orders. When he spoke his voice filled the room.

Notice how *active* the descriptive material is. Instead of saying "Duran has black eyes," Gardner creates movement —"His black eyes gazed vacantly"—giving us the same information but making it more compelling.

Larry L. King uses a similar technique in a profile of

William Buckley he once wrote for *Harper's*. He is describing Buckley standing at a podium, giving a speech.

> His hair is greying (and needs cutting); his skin is weathered, a sailor's. He has, even in clothes newly pressed, a permanently rumpled air. He hunches his shoulders, writhes in his clothes, jams his hands in his back pockets, forcing the pants even lower on his hips and his shirttail out. . . . When he lifts his eyes, it is often to gaze out in a hunched fashion, hands in his pockets, as if staring intently into the ice compartment of a refrigerator.

Notice that even though this is a descriptive paragraph, King relies mainly on verbs—"hunches," "writhes," "jams," etc., to carry his material forward. Too many novice writers seem to think that description is pretty much the job of adjectives and adverbs, but description that is truly vivid is almost always built around active verbs, not adjectives.

Describing People in Depth

I'd like to finish out this section on describing people with two lengthy passages, each of which illustrates not only the descriptive patterns I've been talking about in this chapter but also some of the techniques introduced in earlier chapters. The first passage is Anne Tyler's description of writer Eudora Welty, from the *New York Times Book Review*. The second is Tom Wolfe's description of Ken Kesey, from *The Electric Kool-Aid Acid Test*.

> Her hair is white now and she walks with some care and wears an Ace bandage around her wrist to ease a touch of arthritis. But the eyes are still as luminous as ever, radiating kindness and . . . attention you would have to call it, but attention of a special quality, with some amusement accompanying it. When she laughs, you can see how she must

have looked as a girl—shy and delighted. She will often pause in the middle of a sentence to say, "Oh, I'm just enjoying this so much," and she does seem to be that rare kind of person who takes an active joy in small, present moments. In particular, she is pleased by words, by ways of saying things, snatches of dialogue overheard, objects' names discovered and properly applied. (She likes to read technical manuals and diagrams with the parts labeled. Her whole face lights up when she describes how she heard a country woman confess to a "gnawing and a craving" for something. "Wasn't that a wonderful way of putting it? A gnawing and a craving.")

As we analyze the passage in detail, notice two things in particular: one, the effective mix of factual and impressionistic detail; and, two, the way Ms. Tyler blends her own general observations into the descriptive material.

> Her hair is white now and she walks with some care and wears an Ace bandage around her wrist to ease a touch of arthritis.

Mainly factual detail here but notice how the concrete detail of the "Ace bandage around her wrist" sharpens the picture.

> But the eyes are still as luminous as ever, radiating kindness and . . . attention you would have to call it, but attention of a special quality, with some amusement accompanying it.

This is almost pure impressionistic detail, but it is all the more effective because of the factual detail that precedes it.

> In particular, she is pleased by words, by ways of saying things, snatches of dialogue overheard, objects' names discovered and properly applied. (She likes to read technical manuals and diagrams with the parts labeled. Her whole face lights up when she describes how she heard a country

woman confess to a "gnawing and a craving" for something. "Wasn't that a wonderful way of putting it? A gnawing and a craving.")

Most of the above section consists of details that back up the idea of being "pleased with words." What we have here is more characterization than pure description, but the quote that closes the paragraph could be viewed as description, too. Why is part of the paragraph in parenthesis? Most likely because Ms. Taylor wanted to make a clear distinction between the larger point—Eudora Welty's being pleased by words—and the specific illustrations that back up the point.

Now to Tom Wolfe:

> He [Ken Kesey] is standing with his arms folded over his chest and his eyes focused in the distance, i.e., the wall. He has thick wrists and big forearms, and the way he has them folded makes them look gigantic. He looks taller than he really is, maybe because of his neck. He has a big neck with a pair of sternocleido-mastoid muscles that rise up out of the prison work shirt like a couple of dock ropes. His jaw and chin are massive. He looks a little like Paul Newman, except that he is more muscular, has thicker skin, and he has tight blond curls boiling up around his head. His hair is almost gone on top, but somehow that goes all right with his big neck and general wrestler's build. Then he smiles lightly. It's curious, he doesn't have a line on his face. After all the chasing and hassling, he looks like the third week at the Sauna Spa; serene, as I say.

At first swipe, Wolfe is being himself: chatty, no great concern for the strictures of conventional form. Yet, there *is* form here. As informal and idiomatic as the language is, Wolfe is holding on to our focus and building his description around a balanced mix of factual and impressionistic details. Let's take a closer look.

> He is standing with his arms folded over his chest and his eyes focused in the distance, i.e., the wall.

A screenwriter might call this his opening "long shot." The factual details give the reader a focal point.

> He has thick wrists and big forearms, and the way he has them folded makes them look gigantic.

With our focus already on Kesey's "arms folded over his chest," it's not hard for us to zero in on the "thick wrists" and "big forearms." What's more, Wolfe introduces here the idea that will permeate this description: Kesey's *bigness*. Notice the easy balance of the factual and the impressionistic.

> He looks taller than he really is, maybe because of his neck.

An impressionistic piece of information that pulls our attention from Kesey's arms and wrists and toward his neck. The "maybe because" phrase primes us for details relating to Kesey's neck and why it makes him appear "taller than he really is."

> He has a big neck . . .

Which reinforces "because of his neck."

> . . . with a pair of sternocleido-mastoid muscles that rise up out of the prison work shirt like a couple of dock ropes.

What are "sternocleido-mastoid muscles"? Only an orthopedist would know—or care—but we don't *need* to know since they obviously have to be in the neck. And note the marvelous simile—"like a couple of dock ropes."

> His jaw and chin are massive.

Factual details that carry forward the "bigness" theme.

> He looks a little like Paul Newman, except that he is more muscular, has thicker skin, and he has tight blond curls boiling up around his head.

A quick cut to Paul Newman's face but not for long. The descriptive details that reinforce "except that . . ." move from factual to impressionistic ("tight blond curls boiling up around his head"). We're now back to Kesey's head again.

> His hair is almost gone on top, but somehow that goes all right with his big neck and general wrestler's build.

Recognize the pattern? First a factual detail ("his hair is almost gone on top"), then an observation ("but somehow that goes all right with his big neck"). Note, too, how Wolfe keeps coming back to Kesey's muscularity, his bigness.

> Then he smiles slightly.

A dollop of narrative detail, just in case we're getting a little bored with the description.

> It's curious . . .

(What's curious?)

> . . . he doesn't have a line on his face.

(What's curious about that?)

> After all the chasing and hassling, he looks like the third week at the Sauna Spa; serene, as I say.

An impressionistic image to wind the description up. Camera pulls back. Freeze. Fade-out.

Describing Places and Scenes

Much of what we've just talked about in describing people applies as well to describing places and scenes. The key to effectiveness, once again, is striking the right balance between factual details and impressionistic details. But place and scene description introduces a complication not usually present when you're describing people: guiding your reader's focus. When you're describing a person, the reader automatically connects everything you're saying to the person you're describing; but place and scene descriptions frequently involve different objects in different places. So, apart from making sure that your description is sharp and concrete, you must also make sure that your reader has no trouble *following* your description. Consider this paragraph from William Manchester's *Goodbye, Darkness*. As you read it, note not only how clearly the picture Manchester describes develops in your mind, but how easy it is to follow.

> Streams, the arteries of commerce, support villages at their mouths, often within sight of the beaches. The typical village has a score of well-shaped huts on stilts to provide coolness and protection from floods, the thatched roofs rising high, like hives. Approaching one of them, crossing the Ymi River over a shaky bamboo bridge, my companions and I find beached canoes, dugouts, and frail sampans with rattan hoods. Next we hear the squealing of little black pigs and then the sounds of men and women, all of whom, we discover, are wearing lap shorts. The fishermen, their day's catch in, are asleep on woven mats. Other men, and children, are planting taro, pandanus (screw pines), yams, and sago palms, chanting as they do so. Two young women are nourishing baby pigs. Beside a pile of tropical fruit, which resembles a Ghirlandjo picture, a group of older women are

busy sorting out huge bunches of bananas, bolts of tapa, kava bowls, and necklaces of shells, beads, bones, dog's teeth, sharks' teeth, and, incredibly, Pepsi-Cola bottle caps. Other women are working on stalks of the very useful sago palm; the trunk provides flour for cakes and porridge, and the fabric from the huge branching single flower, twelve feet across, will make bunch skirts which, dyed in rich, deep colors, are worn for festive occasions.

Let's examine more closely how Manchester guides our focus throughout this paragraph. He starts out with "streams" that "support villages," which takes us into a general statement about "the typical village." He narrows our focus in the next sentence with the phrase "Approaching one of them" and introduces himself as a participant in the scene. Look midway in this paragraph at the three sentences that begin with "Two young women" and take us to the end of the paragraph. Notice how Manchester uses "women" as the thread.

The point to remember here is that Manchester makes sure his readers know *what* he is describing before he presents his descriptive details. He is careful, in other words, to *orient* his readers before he shifts focus. We see the same orienting technique in this descriptive paragraph from John Gregory Dunne's essay "Sanctuary." I've italicized the orienting words and phrases—those phrases that direct your focus.

The morning I drove out to Pasadena a barefoot young blond girl was sitting on the steps of the meeting hall, playing a guitar. *Inside,* fifteen or twenty members of the Resistance, some of them with children, were lounging and sleeping in the social room. Most of them were wearing buttons that said CELEBRATE LIFE; BRAHMS NOT BOMBS; and GOD IS AN UNDEFINED TERM. There was turkey soup and hot chocolate and a communal cigarette bowl. *On a bulletin board* was tacked a child's drawing of a peace symbol, around which someone had scrawled, "Jesus wore long hair." *At a table* an intense young woman was addressing Christmas cards; every person on her list was in a federal prison. . . .

Here's yet another example of a descriptive paragraph in which the writer—in this case, Jon Bradshaw—shows concern for his reader's focus. This paragraph comes from a piece called "Savage Skulls," written for *Esquire,* and describes a ride Bradshaw took in a patrol car through "Fort Apache"—the South Bronx—in New York City. Again, I've italicized the orienting phrases.

In spite of the dozens of days I was to spend in Fort Apache, I can still recall the first day with an odd and startling clarity. *We drove through the streets:* nearly every block contained an empty lot or two; the buildings had been burned and razed and the vacant lots were filled with mounds of rubble, garbage, bricks and broken glass. *On the main streets,* between the few occupied buildings, there were gutted bodegas, shops and grocery stores, their scorched and twisted signs still intact. *In block after block,* the burned-out buildings leaned like empty coffins against the more substantial sky. The cratered streets were filled with crippled mongrel dogs. *In the middle of Kelly Street,* a black beggar pushed a grocery cart piled high with wood and copper piping. Dirty children crawled through abandoned cars, stripping them of seats and steering wheels. *On a bridge above the railroad tracks,* a long, narrow sign requested: HELP KEEP HUNTS POINT CLEAN. Someone had added: AND SAFE, but most of the message had been obscured by coarse graffiti.

Artful Description: A Closer Look

Few writers I know handle description better than Paul Theroux, who brings an observant eye and a fresh perspective to nearly everything he writes. The following paragraph, from Theroux's *The Great Railway Bazaar,* seems to me to exemplify descriptive writing that artfully blends factual and impressionistic details and at the same time keeps the reader's focus under control. As you read it, notice how the factual and impressionistic details reinforce one another.

> The lumbering Grand Trunk express that bisects India, a 1400-mile slash from Delhi south to Madras, gets its name from the route. It might easily have derived from the kind of luggage the porters were heaving on board. There were grand trunks all over the platform. I had never seen such heaps of belongings in my life, or so many laden people: they were like evacuees who had been given time to pack, lazily fleeing an ambiguous catastrophe. In the best of times there is nothing simple about an Indian boarding a train, but these people climbing into the Grand Trunk Express looked as if they were setting up house—they had the air, and the merchandise, of people moving in. Within minutes the compartments were colonized, the trunks were emptied, the hampers, food baskets, water bottles, bedrolls, and Gladstones put in place; and before the train started up its character changed, for while we were still standing at Delhi Station the men stripped off their baggy trousers and twill jackets and got into traditional South Indian dress: the sleeveless gym-class undershirt and the sarong they call a *lungi.* These were scored with packing creases. It was as if, at once—in expectation of the train whistle—they all dropped the disguise they had adopted for Delhi, the Madras-bound express allowing them to assume their true identity. The train was full of Tamils; and they had moved in so completely, I felt like a stranger among residents, which was odd, since I had arrived earlier than anyone else.

Let's take a closer look at what makes this passage work.

The lumbering Grand Trunk Express that bisects India, a 1400-mile slash from Delhi south to Madras, gets it name from the route. It might easily have derived it from the kind of luggage the porters were heaving on board. There were grand trunks all over the platform.

Three fairly straightforward sentences, each presenting a single idea that feeds into the idea that follows it. Notice how Theroux takes three sentences to stage this thought. A less accomplished writer might have tried to cram all this information into one or two sentences, perhaps eliminating the third sentence altogether and using "grand trunks" instead of "kind of luggage" in the second sentence. Theroux uses "kind of luggage" as a staging device for the important image here—the "grand trunks all over the platform."

I had never seen such heaps of belongings in my life, or so many laden people: they were like evacuees who had been given time to pack, lazily fleeing an ambiguous catastrophe.

A personal observation spiced with a freshly conceived simile: "evacuees who had been given time to pack, lazily fleeing an ambiguous catastrophe" is an image we can all understand since we've seen it dozens of times on network newscasts.

In the best of times there is nothing simple about an Indian boarding a train, but these people climbing into the Grand Trunk Express looked as if they were setting up house— they had the air, and the merchandise, of people moving in.

In the first part of this sentence, Theroux the observer becomes Theroux the commentator. But he gets us back to the scene quickly, with yet another well-conceived simile that itself consists of a staging phrase ("these people . . . looked as if they were setting up house") and with more specific material to reinforce ("they had the air, and the merchandise, of people moving in").

Within minutes the apartments were colonized, the trunks were emptied, hampers, food baskets, water bottles, bedrolls, and Gladstones put in place; and before the train started up its character changed, for while we were still standing at Delhi Station the men stripped off their baggy trousers and twill jackets and got into traditional South Indian dress: the sleeveless gym-class undershirt and the sarong they call a *lungi*. These were scored with packing creases.

Except for the phrase "the apartments were colonized," this sentence is packed with simple factual details. Theroux's mention of "packing creases" tells us that we're in the hands of a writer with a radarlike eye for detail.

It was as if, at once—in expectation of the whistle—they all dropped the disguise they had adopted for Delhi, the Madras-bound express allowing them to assume their true identity.

This observation is a reflection of Theroux's imagination, but well-written as it is, it wouldn't work as well as it does if not for the concrete details in the two preceding sentences.

The train was full of Tamils; and they had moved in so completely, I felt like a stranger among residents, which was odd, since I had arrived earlier than anyone else.

A factual detail followed by a personal observation closes the paragraph on an arresting note.

Effective Descriptive Writing: A Summary

Let me close out this section on description with some straight nondescriptive tips, all of which we've already touched upon but nonetheless bear repeating.

1. Use a carefully orchestrated mix of factual details and impressionistic details.

2. Keep your reader's focus under control at all times.

3. Wherever possible, mix descriptive details with narrative material.

4. Use figurative devices when they're called for, but use them precisely.

5. Rely less on adjectives and more on active verbs and concrete nouns.

6

Coming to Grips
with Dialogue

IT wasn't too long ago that dialogue writing was considered the province of the playwright and fiction
writer, and nobody expected a writer of nonfiction to be
very good at it. No more. It's the rare feature article today
that doesn't involve quoted material of one kind or another,
and in certain types of articles—profiles and interview
pieces, for instance—you need to be as adept and as versatile in your handling of dialogue as your counterparts in
fiction.

But dialogue writing is by no means an easy skill to
develop. To write convincing dialogue, you need two separate yet related skills. First of all, you need to be sensitive
to the patterns and the rhythms of actual speech—to recognize, for instance, that most people talk in fragments and
not in complete sentences; to recognize, too, that most people express themselves far more idiomatically and simply
when speaking than when writing. At the same time, you
have to master the tricky stylistic problems that arise
whenever you work with dialogue: deciding, for instance,
where to place "he said" or "she said" in a piece of dialogue
(before the quote, after the quote, in the middle of the
quote?); and figuring out how to weave narrative and expository material in and out of your dialogue so that your
dialogue doesn't look as if it belongs in the script for a play.

Don't underestimate the importance of these ancillary

dialogue skills. For in the same way that a little static can go a long way to ruin the pleasure you experience when you listen to a concert on the radio, so can the sloppy handling of the purely mechanical components of dialogue writing go a long way to disrupt the flow—and the effectiveness—of a dialogue passage, regardless of how good an ear you have.

When to Be Direct—and Indirect

You can communicate what people say in two ways: directly and indirectly. And much of your effectiveness as a writer of dialogue will depend on your ability to know when —and how—to use each form. " 'Getting my divorce was the hardest thing I ever had to go through,' admits Jane," is a direct quote. The same statement, in an indirect form, might read as follows: "Jane admits that getting through her divorce was the hardest thing she ever had to go through in her life." (It's possible, too, to combine the two forms, as in, "Jane admits that getting a divorce was the 'hardest thing I had to go through in my life.' ")

The logical question here, of course, is when to use which form, but there is no clear-cut answer. You will usually have a choice between presenting a person's statements in either form, but the choice will rarely be obvious. Direct quotes generally convey a greater sense of authority and immediacy than indirect quotes. What's more, if you orchestrate direct quotes well, you can usually give your reader a more vivid sense of the person you're quoting.

On the other hand, direct quotes aren't always clear enough or succinct enough to get your information across in the most effective way. Most of the time, remember, the people you're quoting won't be as articulate as you are. So if you surrender the burden of communicating entirely to them, you run the risk of losing your reader.

To show you what I mean, let's say you were interviewing a Broadway director and one of the questions you asked was whether this director thought a young person could learn stage directing by taking courses in college. And let's say the answer, once you transcribed it from your tape, came out like this:

> "Well . . . I mean, you can't very well . . . well . . . Jeez, that's tough, you know. I mean, directing plays, you know . . . well, you have to understand, this is *only* an opinion, understand . . . but directing plays, I mean, Christ, you're talking about a damn tough thing to do, you know what I mean. Really, I mean, it's . . . just . . . well, tough."

Or, just as bad, like this:

> "Well, to be sure, one can get a very fine background in the theater in a university, and I would be the last person to discourage anybody from seeking a college education. However, it has always been my feeling that directing is something that one can only learn through direct experience. It's damn tough."

Quoting either of these directors verbatim will accomplish two things, neither of them good. One, you'll embarrass the director; two, you'll chase away readers. So, in this situation, you have little choice but to take responsibility yourself for the quoted material. Here's how you might handle each of the passages.

Revison 1:

Asked whether it's possible to learn in a university setting the skills needed to become a Broadway director, Anderson hedges. "It's tough to say," he says. "Maybe you can, maybe you can't. The thing is, directing plays is a damn tough thing to do. Damn tough."

Revision 2:

Asked whether it's possible to learn in a university setting the skills you need to become a Broadway director, Anderson hedges. He acknowledges that you can get a "fine background in the theater" in a university, and says he would never discourage anybody from seeking a college education. But he feels that directing is something that can be best learned through actual experience. "Directing," he says, "is tough. Damn tough."

We've taken some liberties, it's true. Our director didn't actually come out and say, "It's tough to say." But the revision still represents an *accurate* account of what he said, and the changes seem to me to be not only acceptable but necessary.

I recognize, of course, the ethical question that arises whenever you take it upon yourself to tinker with what somebody else has said, and I don't mean to suggest that you have unlimited license in this regard. If you're going to express in your own words the gist of what somebody has said, or even change things around for clarity, you have to be extremely careful, obviously, not to misrepresent the person you're quoting. And the more sensitive or controversial the subject, the more careful you have to be. I myself have always taken a good deal of liberty with the quoted material I've used in my books and articles, but, then again, I don't generally write about sensitive topics. What's more, I usually make it a practice (and it's a good practice to follow) to get in touch with the people I quote and read them my edited versions of what they said.

Mind you, I'm not advocating that you disregard what your source actually says and make up statements you

think suit the speaker better, but you do have some flexi-
bility—just as long as you don't abuse it.

As far as when to quote someone directly or indirectly is
concerned, there are, as I have said, no hard and fast rules,
but there are a few guidelines to keep in mind—guidelines
that relate, for the most part, to the nature and function of
the quoted material.

For example, the more strictly *informational* the material you're working with is, the better off you are taking
the indirect route—that is, paraphrasing and simplifying,
using direct quotes mainly for emphasis. In the following
example, to illustrate, I've presented as a direct quote information that could be expressed more effectively and succinctly in paraphrase by the writer, as we see in the
revision:

> "I was born and grew up in Chicago," Lucas says. "I went
> to the University of Chicago and when I graduated from the
> University, I immediately went into the army. When I got
> out of the army, I went to work for a small company called
> Weber and Associates. It was a consulting firm that worked
> with banks and brokerage houses. I started off as an assis-
> tant to one of the vice-presidents but worked my way up to
> the vice-presidency myself in five years. I was a vice-presi-
> dent for three years. Once I felt I couldn't move up any
> higher in this company, I decided to start a company of my
> own."

> Lucas was born and grew up in Chicago and attended the
> University of Chicago. As soon as he graduated, he went
> into the army, when he left the army, he went to work for
> Weber and Associates, a small consulting firm whose clients
> included mainly banks and brokerage houses. He started at
> the bottom—as an assistant to one of the vice-presidents—
> and within five years he'd become a vice-president himself.
> But after three years, sensing that he'd never move up any
> higher, he decided to start a company of his own.

In the above examples, the information is the important thing—not the fact that Lucas said it, and not the *way* he said it. Thus there is no need to quote it directly. Of course, if instead of Lucas, we were quoting somebody like Woody Allen or Mel Brooks—or anybody, for that matter, with a genuine gift of gab, we would have good reason for *direct* quotes. Here's a paragraph made up entirely of a direct quote; it's from a piece I wrote many years ago for *Cue* magazine on a woman named Roz Starr, who operated a celebrity information business in New York. I could have presented this same information in *my* words, but Roz Starr had an energetic way of expressing herself, so I was able to present information and at the same time give the reader a sense of Ms. Starr:

> "You have to understand, darling," Roz Starr says, "that celebrities are an industry unto themselves in this town. A big industry. You begin with all the panel and interview shows that originate in the city. Then you've got all the magazines here. And the charities—wow, that's the big part of it. Every charity is looking for celebrities to work on campaigns, and to do benefits. We don't do booking or anything like that. All we do is keep tabs on where everybody is and how they can be reached. In a hurry."

So much for extreme examples. In most situations, you'll find that a combination of the two—direct and indirect—will serve your needs most effectively.

Here's an example of this combination at work in a profile of CBS board chairman William Paley written by Tony Schwartz for the *New York Times Magazine*. In the first half of this paragraph, Schwartz, in his own words, reports the *gist* of what Paley "denies" and "believes," using indirect quotes. The second part of the paragraph is pure quoted material. Conceivably, Schwartz could have used *only* summary or *only* quoted material in this paragraph. The mixture gives the paragraph a sense of movement and immediacy that it wouldn't otherwise have.

Paley denies the suggestion that he is unable to let go gracefully of the corporation he built. He believes that he has simply not been astute in his choices of successors. And because the CBS board of directors remains totally loyal to him, Paley does make the choices. "I'm just a bad picker, I guess," he said. "I thought I had someone good in Arthur Taylor. He was young, articulate, ambitious, aggressive, but he just didn't work out. Some people grow with power, I think, prosper and flower, and some just can't get enough of it. They want more recognition. The title isn't enough. I think that was the case with Taylor."

Notice the order here: indirect quotes in the beginning of the paragraph but the direct quote to close it. This pattern, a series of indirect quotes followed by a direct quote that reinforces or dramatizes the information conveyed in the indirect material, is the pattern favored by most professional writers. The indirect quote primes the reader for the direct quote that follows. Some examples:

The developer believes there is a simple reason why he is able to see things that others cannot, why he can build a waterslide that is aesthetically pleasing, or put up an artificial lighthouse that becomes a tourist attraction. "I'm richly endowed with a rare treasure of mental images," he says. "The process is: stock my brain, stock my brain, stock my brain."

Alice concedes that she is a difficult woman to work with and doesn't deny that on occasion she is abusive to the people who work under her. On the other hand, she insists that she has always been concerned about the welfare of her subordinates. "Everybody who works for me," she says, "knows that when they're in trouble they can come to me, and I'll always help them."

Nothing fancy here. The indirectly quoted material in both cases supplies information quickly and succinctly. The quotes in both cases are *directly keyed* to the earlier material. A *direct* connection between indirectly quoted material and the quoted material that follows is crucial. Your readers will automatically assume that any direct quote following an indirect quote will be connected to that quote. Break the pattern and you'll jar the reader's focus. So, whenever you want a direct quote to introduce a *new* focus or to give the reader a different perspective on a previously introduced point, you need a transitional phrase. You'll see why when you compare the following passages with two possible revisions.

> Merton admits freely that he is a workaholic and doesn't need recreational pursuits to keep him relaxed. "I like sailing," he says. "It's an interesting sport, and I've been doing it for years. I've won a few cups and I enjoy racing. I've owned three different sail boats. But I don't *have* to sail to unwind."

When you write that someone freely admits "he is a workaholic and doesn't need recreational pursuits to keep him relaxed," you prime your reader for a quote that will back up that statement. The writer here eventually backs up the statement, but waits too long. Until the last statement, the quote seems to contradict the opening statement about Merton. Here are two different ways of correcting the problem:

> Merton admits freely that he is a workaholic and doesn't need recreational pursuits to keep him relaxed. "I like sailing," he says, "but I don't have to sail to unwind."

In this revision, we've eliminated the little thoughts ("it's an interesting sport," "I've been doing it for years," etc.)

because they serve only to reinforce a point that the last
sentence is going to contradict anyway.

> Merton admits freely that he is a workaholic and doesn't
> need recreational pursuits to keep him relaxed. He does,
> however, sail and has been a successful sailboat racer. "I
> like sailing," he says. "But I don't *have* to sail to unwind.

The "however" in the second sentence prepares us for the
information on sailing which otherwise would have come
as a surprise. Notice how the last quote addresses both the
second sentence—Merton's interest in sailing—and the
main point of the paragraph, which is that Merton doesn't
need recreational pursuits to relax.

Integrating Quotes with other Material

Long stretches of quoted material are tedious to read, regardless of how interesting the quotes. So it's generally a
good practice, when possible, to integrate quotes with ex-
position, narrative, or description. In the following passage
from a *Sports Illustrated* profile by Jim Kaplan of tennis
player Leslie Allen, notice how the quotes relate logically
to the biographical details that precede them.

> Leslie caught the tennis bug for good as a high school senior
> in Cleveland, where she was living at the time with her
> father, Howard. "I was too tall to be a cheerleader; I couldn't
> sing and couldn't twirl a baton," she says. "There was noth-
> ing for me to do, and I didn't want to sit around and watch
> TV." But it wasn't until the end of her freshman year at
> Pittsburgh's Carnegie Mellon Institute that she settled on
> the game as a career. "She glibly announced, 'I want to play
> professionally,' without having shown she had the slightest
> bit of talent," says her mother. "So we decided to take it step
> by step, on a five-year plan."

Here's another example of the same technique, from an article I wrote in the mid-1960s for *Playbill* on the wardrobe mistress of the New York City Ballet. Notice how all the biographical details culminate in the final quote at the end.

> Asked to recall some of the more memorable experiences of her life, Madame Pourmel shrugs and tells you there are too many. Yet, little things stay fixed in her memory. She can recall one particular day during World War II (when the Ballet Russe de Monte Carlo was touring under some of the most adverse conditions imaginable) hearing a little boy exclaim, as she was unpacking costumes in a dimly lit gymnasium, "Hey, we're having another rummage sale." Far worse is the memory of a drizzly morning in San Diego not too long afterward. At the time she was keenly worried about her mother in Leningrad and her brothers in France, not to mention her husband, who was somewhere with the French underground and unable to send any message to her as to his welfare. "It's silly," she says, "but I'll never forget that day. I was having coffee in a little luncheonette, and the coffee was so bad I couldn't drink it. So I asked the waitress, please, could I have a little sugar. And she looked at me, with almost hate in her eyes, and said, 'Don't you know there's a war on?' as if I needed to be reminded of it. I can still picture her face."

The basic function of each of the paragraphs just covered was to provide biographical information, so the quoted material, along with the other information, is sufficient to do the job. Frequently, though, when you're recreating a specific incident or scene in which you're using quotes, you may want to inject additional immediacy into your material, which means you have to include narrative or descriptive details.

Here, from a *Newsweek* piece, is how one writer effectively combines direct quotes, indirect quotes, and brief narrative details to give the paragraph a compelling immediacy.

Scene Nine. To demonstrate the marvels of his new studio, Coppola holds a press conference complete with a $13,000 catered lunch for the reporters. Standing in front of a neon "Lady Luck" sign, he talks about his money woes: "I didn't count on the very drastic change in the climate in Hollywood today," he says, referring to the industry's new tight-fistedness in the wake of the *Heaven's Gate* disaster. Yes, he has had to lay off his story department and he mourns that "we had our electronic-research budget cut entirely. . . . What the banks want from me," he says, "is my studio. A bank has one objective only: to make their money safe. So they don't care whether I build the greatest studio in the world next year. They want to know about next Monday." How will he make *One from the Heart* and keep Zoetrope together? "One step at a time," he says. "That's the only way when you're walking into no man's land." Gesturing to the surrounding wonders, Coppola sums up: "I just want you to see that we've done what I promised."

Here's an even more vivid example of the same technique, from a Rex Reed profile of actress Irene Papas.

As long as she talks about Greece, the eyes glow with some of the grandeur of Clytemnestra. But when the topic turns to Irene Papas, she winces and the eyes become sad, misshapen bullets, avoiding the issue. "Oh, how I hate to be charming for interviews. I never believed publicity had anything to do with acting. I don't believe people want to really know about me. Maybe if I liked myself more as a person, I would not mind talking about myself. But I am very vulnerable and open and it's up to you what you do with me. You can hang me in the paper if you want, but I will try to be a good interview for you and tell you what you ask." She stabs a pork chop with a sullen fork and takes a deep breath. "My childhood?" A smile, and the corners of her dark mouth turn into a cave of secrets. "That was a happy time in Greece. I come from a village 100 kilometers from Athens called Chi-liomodion." She writes it on the tablecloth in Greek letters for me. "A tiny village, very ugly, but we have a telephone in our house and electricity. My family were teachers. My father is 96 now, on the pension. My mother, who is 66, lives in New York with me. I don't want her to go back now while the junta is there."

Worth pointing out here is the strategic placement of the narrative and descriptive details. Reed doesn't lump them all together. Instead he intersperses them throughout the paragraph. This shift from what people are saying to what they're doing *when* they say it, is essentially a pacing device. It enhances the impact of the quoted material and it gives the reader a stronger sense of the person doing the talking.

When More Than One Person Is Talking

Introduce more than one person in any piece you're writing, and your dialogue problems become more complicated. First of all, you have to constantly make sure that you keep straight in your reader's mind *who* is saying *what*. Secondly, interweaving narrative and descriptive details into the dialogue becomes all the trickier.

One of the best ways I can think of to develop the skills you need to handle conversation with assurance is to read and reread dialogue passages in nonfiction that look and sound as if they would fit into a well-written novel or short story. You need to develop a certain "feel" for when—and where—to inject a narrative detail or descriptive, and this "feel" is best gained through osmosis. One of the things I did years ago that helped me learn how to write conversational scenes was to analyze passages from writers who handled such scenes very well and then use exactly the

same patterns to construct scenes of my own. Take the following dialogue, from Norman Mailer's *The Armies of the
Night.*

> After the conversation with Macdonald, he had a short
> word with Lowell.
> "Hungover?" Lowell had asked, after a pause.
> "Pretty bad."
> Lowell gave a commiserative nod. Then next he asked
> casually, studying Mailer, "See the papers?"
> "Yes."
> "Not so nice."
> "I guess not. They'll be worse," said Mailer.

Analyzing each paragraph, we find the following pattern:

¶1. Single sentence with narrative information.

¶2. Dialogue, followed by "had asked," followed by ad-
verbial phrase.

¶3. Reply to quote.

¶4. Narrative detail ("Lowell gave a commiserative
nod"), followed by dialogue, introduced by "Then he
asked . . . ."

¶5. Dialogue.

¶6. Dialogue.

¶7. Dialogue, followed by "said Mailer."

Using this pattern as a model, you can then write your
own paragrpah.

> After his talk with the Board, Peters had a brief chat
> with Nicholson.
> "Bad news, huh?" Nicholson had asked, after a moment
> or so.
> "Not good."
> Peterson shook his head. Then he asked quietly, looking
> down, "Have you seen the latest figures?"
> "Yes."

"Pretty bad, huh?"

"Well, they could be worse," said Pete.

The number of different patterns you'll uncover when you do this exercise is almost infinite, but don't approach the exercise with the idea of *mastering* specific patterns. The idea, simply, is to imitate as many as you can so that you yourself can begin to get a sense of the possibilities. Here are a few examples to get you started.

From Frank Conroy's *Stop-Time:*

> The flat, green Jersey meadows slipped by outside, wiped every few seconds by the dark blur of a telephone pole.
>
> "I ran away when I was seventeen," he said suddenly, after miles of silence. "I never went back."
>
> My head whipped around. "You did?" It seemed an incredible coincidence, but I believed him.
>
> "My old man was a bastard." A faint smile appeared on his face. "He beat us up all the time. Best thing I ever did was leave."
>
> "Where'd you go?"
>
> "One morning he came at me in the barn and before I knew it, I laid him out with a pitchfork. Wham! Right on the ear." The smile was broader now. "He went down like a tree. I thought sure he was dead but of course he wasn't. Just out cold." He laughed. "I didn't wait for him to come around, though. No sir, I left immediately."

Note how brief the sentences are that narrate action. These little action bits back up the dialogue, they don't interfere with it.

From Rex Reed's profile of Simone Signoret:

> "Don't tell me your name," she says, "because I am French and we never hear names. It will just go right in one ear and out the other. I will just call you Mr. New York Times. This is David Warner." Warner, who starred in *Morgan* and now plays the very British-sounding Russian son of the very French-sounding Signoret in *The Sea Gull,* extends

a limp hand. "I hate this room. They didn't want to let me in without a tie," he says, shaking his hair, which is long enough to braid, and blinking his eyes nervously behind oblong glasses thick enough to see the moon through. Signoret then introduces Mrs. Warner, a round-faced young Swedish morsel who looks like a stand-in for *Candy,* and Moura Budberg, an elderly Russian dowager who translated and adapted the film version of Chekhov's play. Miss Budberg stares coldly at the intruder from a hooded cape, looking very much like an old photo of Isak Dinesen. "The old hag claims to be a baroness," says Signoret, "but we all suspect her of being an old Russian phony." Miss Budberg cackles, enjoying the insult. They've all been drinking several bottles of white wine and they're all a bit smashed.

From Harry Stein's *Esquire* piece, "The Eternal Jocks":

Bandy responds with a defiant sweep of his hand, taking in the picnic area, the tavern, the field in the blackness beyond. "Everybody's saying Holdt is finished. Well, I like that they're saying it. It'll make 'em easier to beat."

"Hell, I'm not ready to quit yet," agrees Spearman. He glances at DePalma. "Me and June, we plan to keep on going. Ain't that right, June?"

"Into my forties, fifties, sixties . . ."

Bandy thinks a moment. "I'll definitely keep playing at least until my five-year-old son starts. Maybe then I'll go into coaching Little League or something."

"You know," says Junior with a small smile, "between your kid and Richie's kid and Jo Jo's two kids, we're gonna have a whole team pretty soon."

The More "Saids" the Better

In case you didn't notice in the paragraphs above, none of the writers had any compunctions at all about using the word "says" or "said." This alone differentiates them from many inexperienced writers.

I have nothing against an occasional "asked" (or "asks"), "answered," "replied," "exclaimed," but plenty against forced synonyms like "queried," "inquired of," "rejoined," and, heaven forbid, nonwords like "enthused" (as in, " 'We're going tomorrow,' enthused Bonnie"). I don't mind an occasional " 'I feel bad,' sighed Charlie" but I don't like " 'I feel terrific,' *smiled* Charlie." Words that describe how a person talks, like "piped" or "chimed," are okay, but don't overdo them. And while we're on the subject of overdoing things, watch out for superfluous adverbs—adverbs that aren't needed to get your point across, such as in " 'I love you,' he said tenderly," which is a first cousin to " 'I hate you,' she said hatefully."

The Who Said What—and When— Dilemma

The placement of the two or three words that indicate who, exactly, is speaking is one of the trickier aspects of dialogue writing. The rule: never leave doubt in the reader's mind as to *who* is saying *what*. Some contemporary fiction writers have a habit of omitting any reference to the speaker, even where the dialogue bounces back and forth a dozen times. *If* the writer is skillful enough, a reader can tell by the way something is being said who's saying it. Sometimes, though, I find myself counting back to the last reference point, which is troublesome for me because I am a sloppy counter. Some writers *always* indicate the speaker, either be inserting "he said," or something akin to it, or by preceding a piece of dialogue with a brief slice of narrative —"Frank raised his eyebrows"—that puts the focus on the speaker. Other writers will allow dialogue to go naked if "he said" or an indication of action, gesture, etc., isn't necessary. Look at the following exchange from one of my own pieces.

> After rehearsal, I approached Frank Corsaro, who had been watching from the back of the darkened theater.
> "Well, I did it," I said.
> "Pardon me," Corsaro replied.
> "I found an identity for my character," I told him. "Like we talked about yesterday."
> "Oh, yes! Yes!" Corsaro said. "Now I remember. Why, that's marvelous."
> "His name is Pietro," I said.
> "Pietro."
> "Yes," I said. "I named him after Mascagni, the composer. I think he would have been pleased."
> "I'm sure," Corsaro said. "So you're feeling better, yes?"
> "Yes," I said. "Much better."
> "Good. That's very good."

In two of the lines of dialogue above, you'll see no mention of a speaker. Yet it's clear in both cases who is speaking. The rule to follow is this: if you send a piece of dialogue out there naked, make sure you quickly identify the speaker in the *next* piece of dialogue.

Notice, too, that the "I said" or "Corsaro replied . . . said" phrases frequently appear in the middle of the sentence instead of at the end or beginning. Deciding where to insert phrases is largely a matter of ear—how the dialogue flows. A good rule of thumb is to insert the phrase in between two separate thoughts. Where you put the "I said," or whatever you're inserting, will shade the meaning of the statement, so you have to experiment. Consider the following:

> "Yes," I said. "I named him after Mascagni, the composer. I think he would have been pleased."

Inserting "I said" after "Yes" gives more impact to the reply. It sets it off from the rest of the sentence. Compare the placement of "I said" in each of the following:

> I said: "Yes, I named him after Mascagni, the composer. I think he would have been pleased."

> "Yes, I named him after Mascagni, the composer. I think he would have been pleased," I said.

Neither of these versions works as well as the original, and the reason lies in the pacing of the quote. The following version represents an improvement on the previous two but changes the emphasis:

> "Yes. I named him after Mascagni, the composer," I said. "I think he would have been pleased."

If there is a "rule" here—and I'm not sure there is—it's this: insert "I said" (or whatever) immediately after that portion of the quote you want to emphasize more than any other.

7

Polishing Up Your Basic Skills

I haven't devoted much space in this book (as you've un-doubtedly noticed) to the so-called mechanics of writing —not because I don't consider mechanics important but because I don't think the ability to deftly handle the ba-sics of grammar and composition is what distinguishes accomplished writers from mediocre ones. Besides, there are a number of excellent books on the market that deal with the purely mechanical aspects of writing. The terri-tory has been well mined, to say the least.

All the same, you can't expect to survive as a professional writer unless your fundamentals are solid. So what I'd like to do in this chapter is to focus on those aspects of mechan-ics that persistently cause problems for most novice and intermediate writers.

The Anatomy of Good Sentences

Sentence writing warrants a book unto itself, so I'm not going to sermonize about how important it is that you keep your sentences as brief as possible (within reason), that you keep your construction parallel and your tenses consistent, and that you do what you can to keep the mechanical work-ings of your sentences from interfering with your reader's ability to figure out what you're trying to say. Here are three principles of effective construction that are easy to remember and surprisingly useful if you can keep them in mind as you write.

1. Keep your subject and verb as close together as possible.

Get into the habit—and it's an easy enough habit to develop—of thinking *verb* every time you write down the subject of a sentence, and you'll be surprised at how much sharper your sentences become. True, there are exceptions to the rule—situations in which you'll deliberately separate the subject and the verb to achieve a particular effect —but as a general rule try to make the subject–verb connection in your sentences as direct as possible.

To prove my point—here's a paragraph out of Michael Korda's book, *Success!* Korda, whom I've already quoted in this book, is an unusually fluid writer: his material *moves.* So let's read through the following paragraph, noting as we go the number of words that separate each subject from the verb that relates to it.

Admittedly a rather special and minor industry, book *publishing* nonetheless *provides* some interesting insights into the dynamics of women in business. Originally, *publishing was* a male dominated business. Rather old fashioned and paternalistic, *it consisted* mostly of small privately owned family companies competing against each other in a very limited and "gentlemanly" way. The *executives, owners, managers* and *editors were* always men, while the *secretaries were* invariably women. Very often the daughters of men in the upper ranks of publishing, these *women had* college degrees and "good" family backgrounds. The book *business hit* the technological revolution very late, with the result that *firms merged, families sold out* to entrepreneurs, and *these* in turn later *sold out* to conglomerates. *What had been* a small cottage industry *became* a large and very profitable business.

Observe how much easier it is to read the Korda passage than to read the following paragraph, written by a member of Congress and printed on the Op-Ed page of the *New York Times*. As I did with the Korda paragraph, I've italicized the subject and verb.

> A *decision* by Mr. Reagan to acquiesce in the abandonment of an internationally acceptable agreement *would have* seriously adverse consequences not only for our African diplomacy but also for our alliance relationships as well. Our British and West German *allies,* with whom we have worked on the Namibian problem, *would be* deeply *disturbed* if we undermined the talks. *Mr. Reagan has* frequently *addressed* the need to strengthen the western alliance, and any unilateral American *repudiation* of the Eastern and United Nations initiatives on Namibia *would* hardly *augur* well for Western European cooperation on such issues as the Persian Gulf and North Atlantic Treaty Organization defense expenditures.

Unfortunately, getting the subject and the verb closer in the above sentences is more than a matter of shoving the in-between words aside. The sentences in question, in fact, suffer from a more fundamental problem, the nature of which we'll look at later in this chapter when we talk about nouns doing the work that active verbs should be doing.

2. Avoid the passive voice whenever possible.

The passive voice is so frequently an object of attack in writing books, my impulse is to defend it simply out of pity. But the fact remains that the passive voice is a more than infrequent culprit in awkward and wordy sentences (particularly in business writing) and there isn't much to be said in its defense. Apart from being an unnatural way of expressing yourself (hardly anybody *speaks* in the passive voice), the passive voice almost invariably weakens a sentence because it (1) almost invariably weakens the verb, and (2) lengthens the sentence by obliging you to add qualifying details in the form of infinitives or prepositional phrases.

The distinction between the two voices, active and passive, is easy enough to make. The way you "passify" a verb is to start out with some form of the auxiliary "to be" and follow the auxiliary with the past participle of the verb. What this does is make what would normally be the subject of an active verb the *receiver* of the action. So, instead of "Charlie drove the car," which is active, you end up with "the car was driven by Charlie." Instead of "Everybody had a good time," you get "A good time was had by all."

Sometimes, of course, for clarity or for emphasis, you can use the passive voice legitimately. Look at the following sentence:

> The ball Jackson hit traveled more than 450 feet and landed in the last row of the right-field bleachers where it was retrieved by a twelve-year-old who admitted later he wasn't even a Yankee fan.

The passive section of this sentence ("where it was retrieved by") could have been expressed in the active voice (and, by the way, I've just slipped into the passive voice in this sentence), but this would have disrupted the rhythm of the sentence and shifted the reader's focus away from the ball. So it *is* possible to use the passive voice to improve the readability of your writing, just as it is also possible, sometimes, to walk through poison ivy without getting a terrible rash. The fact is, however, that even in those situations in which you can get away with the passive voice, the active voice generally works better. The reason is that the reader prefers to find out who or what is doing the action before he learns what has been done and to whom.

Here are examples of sentences, most from student papers, burdened with the inappropriate use of the passive voice, each revised to change the voice to active and thus imbue the sentences with more energy.

(a) Agreement has already been expressed by the three presidential candidates on the format of the debate.
(b) The three presidential candidates have already agreed on the debate format.

(a) The concept of the literary hero can be seen to date back to ancient Greece.
(b) The concept of the literary hero dates back to ancient Greece.

(a) It has been brought to my attention that yesterday there was another incident in the cafeteria.
(b) I've just learned that yesterday another incident took place in the cafeteria.

(a) The decision was made to favor the new proposal.
(b) We decided in favor of the new proposal.

3. Use Dependent Clauses with Care

As you undoubtedly learned in grade school, any sentence in which there is a dependent clause—i.e., a clause that needs an independent clause if it is to make any sense —is known as a complex sentence. In most accomplished nonfiction writing, complex sentences usually outnumber simple sentences and compound sentences, which is why I would never discourage you from expressing your thoughts in complex sentences. Keep in mind, however, that dependent clauses can get you into all kinds of trouble if you're not careful how you use them and where you place them. This is particularly true of *introductory* dependent clauses.

There is, however, a simple way to prevent an introductory dependent clause from creating problems and that is to use dependent clauses sparingly as sentence openers. Your readers won't mind. Indeed, you do your readers a favor when you place the main subject and verb of your sentence as close to the beginning as possible, for once your reader knows where you're taking him in a sentence, he can sit back and enjoy the ride. I'm not saying to begin *all* your sentences with the same subject–verb pattern, but don't go out of your way to *avoid* the pattern simply to make your presentation more—well, *impressive*. Look at the following paragraph from E. B. White's essay "A Report in Spring."

> Mice have eaten the crowns of the Canterbury bells, my white-faced steer has warts on his neck (I'm told it's a virus, like everything else these days), and the dwarf pear has bark trouble. My puppy has no bark trouble. He arises at three, for tennis. The puppy's health, in fact, is exceptionally good. When my wife and I took him from the kennel, a week ago today, his mother kissed all three of us good-bye, and the lady who ran the establishment presented me with complete feeding instructions, which included a mineral supplement called Pervinal and some vitamin drops called Vi-syneral. But I knew that so soon as the puppy reached home and got his sea legs he would switch to the supplement du jour—a flake of well-rotted cow manure from my boot, a dead crocus bulb from the lawn, a shingle from the kindling box, a bloody feather from the execution block behind the barn. Time has borne me out; the puppy was not long in discovering the delicious supplements of the farm, and he now knows where every vitamin hides, under its stone, under its loose board. I even introduced him to the tonic smell of coon.

This paragraph consists of eight sentences and only one of them ("When my wife and I took him from the kennel . . .") starts with an introductory clause.

Not that introductory constructions aren't useful in certain situations. The point, though, is to use them judiciously, and mainly as a means of giving your sentence rhythms added variety. And when you *do* precede your main subject with an introductory group of words, be sure you don't nudge the reader's focus away from the subject. Here are some student examples in which carelessly written introductory expressions produce confusion.

> In order to rectify the situation, employees who continue to operate in a slipshod manner will be fined.

The way this is written, it looks as if the employees are going to rectify the situation. Better:

> In order to rectify the situation, we intend to fine any employees who operate in a slipshod manner.

Here's a more complex example:

> Although some thought that Hagler might be confused by Minter's ability to keep opponents away with that quick jab and left cross, Hagler soon ignored these minor irritations and began throwing bombs from both sides.

Confusion. It seems as if the "minor irritations" ignored by Hagler refer to the fact that "some [people] thought" Hagler might be confused by Minter. That's the impression "although" creates. The revision:

> Some thought that Minter's ability to keep his opponents at bay with his quick jab and left cross might confuse Hagler, but Hagler had no problem infiltrating Minter's defenses and shortly after the opening bell began throwing bombs from both sides.

Example number three:

> Upon arrival, not only was the parking lot full, but the waiting line was a mile long, extending out to the boardwalk onto the sea.

The parking lot didn't arrive, the writer did. And while we're at it, be careful of "not only." To say "not only was the parking lot full" leads us to expect some comment that relates specifically to the parking lot being full, such as "Not only was the parking full, but the cars were jammed in so tightly I couldn't imagine how anybody was going to get out." You not only don't *need* "not only" in this sentence, you don't want it either. The correction:

> When I got there, the parking lot had long since filled up, and the waiting line of cars, stretching along the board-walk, seemed a mile long.

Finally:

> If you are a temporary, part-time employee, a good review could mean we could increase your wages and be more likely to offer you a job in the future.

The correction:

> If we are pleased with your performance as a temporary, part-time employee, we will increase your wages and perhaps offer you a full-time job.

Putting Lazy Verbs to Work

When you encounter lethargic, hard-to-digest writing, you find almost invariably that the verbs are not doing what most verbs are supposed to do: express direct action. Instead, that function has been taken over by nouns, adjectives, or nondirect action verb forms such as infinitives. Here's a classic example, from an already quoted Op-Ed page piece in the *New York Times.*

> A successful conclusion to the Namibian negotiations, on the other hand, is likely to result in a diminution or elimination of the Cuban troop presence in Angola.

The only verb in this long-winded sentence is "is." But there are four nouns that *suggest* action: the nouns "conclusion," "negotiations," "diminution," and "elimination," and one phrase, "likely to result," that does the same thing. It isn't necessary to activate all of these would-be verbs to produce a sentence with more clarity and vigor, but look how much better the sentence reads when you activate just three of them.

> Bringing the Namibian negotiations to a successful conclusion could diminish or maybe even eliminate the Cuban troop presence in Angola.

Here's another sentence from the same article. I've italicized the words that conceal would-be active verbs.

> A *decision* by Mr. Reagan *to acquiesce* in the *abandonment* of an internationally acceptable agreement would have seriously adverse consequences not only for our African diplomacy but also for our alliance relationships as well.

Here, again, a long and awkward sentence with only one pure verb—"would have"—and a weak verb at that. Look at the same sentence with the action expressed through verbs or infinitives.

> Should Mr. Reagan decide to abandon an internationally acceptable agreement, it could hurt not only our African diplomacy but our alliance relationships as well.

From student papers, here are some illustrations of the same problem and the change that corrected the problem:

> One occupational hazard is the spoilage of meat during the summer months.

"Spoilage of meat" will never do. Can you imagine your neighborhood butcher telling an employer, "Be careful that the spoilage of meat doesn't occur"? The sentence reads better as:

Meat spoils during the summer months if you're not careful.

In the following, the use of nouns flattens the impact:

Physical appearance is important. Weight control, attractive dress, and cosmetic improvement will boost your morale.

The writer of this sentence obviously wanted to stress the importance of weight, dress, and makeup, but he could have put his points across with considerably more punch by using active verbs.

It's important to keep up your physical appearance. Watch your weight. Dress attractively. Apply your cosmetics with care.

Another sentence in which action is submerged, followed by a more vigorous revision:

This is best accomplished by the diligent rubbing of the area with a piece of soft toweling.
To get the best results, rub the area diligently with a piece of soft toweling.

I have what I think is a foolproof method to endow you overnight with a bloodhound's nose for altered and concealed verbs: keep an eye peeled for sentences that contain more than their share of "-ing" and "-tion" words and more than one or two prepositions, especially the preposition, "of." Indeed, if the word preceding "of" ends in "-tion" you can almost always shoot first and ask questions later. Some examples of weak sentences and their revised forms:

(a) The addition of Lester James to our staff has been instrumental in the creation of a higher sense of morale in the department.
(b) Since Lester James joined our staff, our morale has risen noticeably.

(a) The implementation of this plan is important to the success of our company.

(b) If we are to succeed, we must implement this plan.

(a) Our assessment of the situation has brought about a realization regarding the seriousness of our problem.

(b) We have assessed the situation and it looks like we're up the creek without a paddle.

If you still question the damage you can do to your writing by using nouns, adjectives, and "of" phrases instead of verbs, look at what happens when you take a piece of writing laced with strong, active verbs and reverse the process I've been talking about—that is, turn the verbs into noun and adjective forms. The following paragraph comes from a *Sports Illustrated* profile of tennis coach Vic Braden by Frank Deford, a fine writer who would rather dance barefoot on spikes than burden his readers with lethargic prose. Read the paragraph as it was *originally* written and then read the weakened version.

A classic figure of modern American myth is the beautiful girl who suddenly discovers that she is beautiful. Usually this occurs when somebody takes off her eyeglasses or her hair tumbles down or some such thing. This happened to Braden—with regard to his brain. One day, as if the Wizard of Oz had handed him a diploma, he found out that he had a brain, and that revelation still thrills and warms him. Also, this happened, indirectly, because of tennis, and as a consequence he not only thinks about thinking all the time, but he feels a certain gratitude to tennis.

Now we get rid of all those crisp, active verbs and replace them with weaker ones and/or nouns and adjectives, plus plenty of "of" phrases:

A classic figure of modern American myth is the beautiful girl who comes to the sudden discovery that she is beautiful. Usually this occurrence takes place with the taking off of her glasses or the tumbling down of her hair or some such thing. A happening of this nature affected Braden—with regard to his brain. One day, as if the Wizard of Oz had blessed him with the handing to him of a diploma, he came to the realization that he was the possessor of a brain, and it was the revelation of this that had a thrilling and warming effect on him. Also, the occurrence of this was due, indirectly, to tennis, and as a consequence, his thoughts about tennis are also marked with a feeling of gratitude that he has toward tennis.

The prosecution rests.

Slimming Down "Fat" Writing

"Fat" writing is the term I use to describe writing in which there are too many words that don't do any work except to make the going tougher and slower for your readers. Your reader's brain, remember, doesn't know until *after* it's processed and tried to connect a word or a phrase whether that word or phrase was absolutely essential, and by that time it's already too late. "Fat" writing makes your readers tired. And sometimes grouchy. Here's the kind of writing I'm talking about:

> In attempting to briefly, yet concisely, explain this process, it becomes necessary to define certain established premises. As most will concur, the primary object is in fact to communicate the message, at all levels.

Here's a writer who obviously likes the sound of his own voice. Why else would he not express the same ideas much more plainly? Why would he add "yet concisely" after briefly? Don't they mean the same thing? Why wouldn't he write this the way he might have said it—simply and plainly, as follows:

To explain the concept, we need a premise: the object of writing is to communicate a message.

Here's another example of fat writing:

> My only reservation comes from a feeling that this result is lacking in the subtleties that make it felt or believable. This may be the reason that I feel the task of writing something on the order of a short story or magazine article would be biting off more than I can chew.

Let's slim this passage down part by part: Instead of "My only reservation comes from a feeling that . . .," say "What troubles me is . . ." Instead of "this result is lacking in the subtleties that make it felt or believable," say "lacks subtlety." Instead of "This may be the reason that I feel the task of writing . . ." say "This is why writing a short story or magazine article seems to me to be biting off more than I can chew."

I don't mean to suggest that this kind of revising is easy. It's not. Nor is revising a skill I can teach you in a few paragraphs. But here are four principles you should file in your mind and never forget:

1. Don't use two or three words when one word will do.
2. Don't use big words when little words will do.
3. Don't use noun phrases instead of active verbs (i.e., don't say, "I have the capability of doing" instead of "I can").
4. Don't write anything you wouldn't be comfortable *saying*.

The "Homeless" Pronoun

Substituting a pronoun—"it," "he," "she," "this," etc.—for a noun or a phrase is a common, and certainly useful, device for enhancing the readability of your prose, but it's a riskier business than most people realize, and there's no way you can be *too* careful about making certain you leave no doubt in your reader's mind about what the pronoun refers to. Consider the following examples:

> Get the feel of the wheel. It is one of the most important instruments in driving a car. With this wheel, you will steer the car when it is in motion.

The first "it" refers back to the wheel. No problem. But having already associated "it" with wheel, our inclination is to associate the second "it" with wheel as well, even though the writer wanted to refer to "car."

> Commuters might be receptive to periodic fare increases if Conrail's service increased as well, but this will probably never happen.

What does "this" refer to? Does it refer to the fact that commuters might be receptive to periodic fare increases, or that Conrail will never improve its service?

The rule here is simple. Whenever you find yourself about to use a pronoun, check—*at that moment*—if using that pronoun will create doubt in the reader's mind about what you're referring to. If there is even a slight chance of doubt, make whatever change is necessary to keep your meaning clear.

Closing on a Solid Note

It's a basic axiom of good composition that the most important ideas or images in the sentence belong either at the beginning or at the end, which would make these ideas or images either the first or the last things your reader registers. Let me amend this axiom to suggest that whenever you have a choice, try to end your sentences with either a noun or a noun phrase—something solid for your reader to focus on before moving on to a new sentence. Compare the following sentences that don't follow this principle with the revisions, which merely alter the endings.

(a) The Masterweaver is a revolutionary handweaving loom that takes only ten minutes to set up.
(b) The Masterweaver is a revolutionary handweaving loom you can set up in only ten minutes.

The slight change here gives added emphasis to "only ten minutes."

(a) French law prohibits the sale of any cognac with a vintage date because of rampant abuse of age claims some years ago.
(b) French law prohibits the sale of any cognac with a vintage date because some years ago several vintners made it their practice to lie about the dates.

Notice that we've not only changed the ending here, we've given the sentence more impact by expressing the second half of the sentence in a more active form.

(a) Being a shoreline community, Fairfield has a luxury some of our neighboring towns do not.
(b) Being a shoreline community, Fairfield has a luxury not enjoyed by our neighboring towns.

If you take the time to do some counting, you'll find that most sentences in the work of the more technically proficient nonfiction writers end with a noun or noun phrase. Here's a paragraph from Peter Schrag's *The Decline of the WASP* that is by no means atypical.

We all know what happened to it, there is no point in reciting again the history of a despair that refuses to fade from memory. But despair is not all that was left. Even with the failures of the sixties the genie wouldn't go back into the bottle. Black power was emulated by Puerto Rican

Power, the Panthers (succeeding the muslims in the night-mares of J. Edgar Hoover) were emulated by the Young Lords, and by a series of newly self-conscious ethnic move-ments. Bilingual classes (in English and Spanish) had be-come fashionable not only in the major cities but in parts of the Southwest, black studies were a fact (if sometimes also a travesty), and the sachems of culture were predominantly people of a new breed. Most of all, the young had suddenly become a force. If the sixties taught us all about the inade-quacies of the old mainstream without solving them, the decade did send people marching to a new tune, and most of all to a new beat.

8

The Professional Difference

ONE night several years ago I found myself seated at a dinner party beside a woman who talked almost non-stop for an hour and a half about her son's exploits in Pee Wee hockey. Hockey is not a great passion of mine, but had the woman at least *attempted* to make her presentation entertaining, it might not have been such a struggle for me to keep my eyes open. She didn't. Too many writers, I'm afraid, are guilty of the same crime: they assume, *a priori,* that their readers have an abiding interest in what they're writing and they take no trouble to make their presentation lively and engaging. They feel no obligation whatsoever to show their readers a good time.

Not so the top echelon of professional writers, and not so aspiring writers who are likely to reach that echelon. What differentiates these writers from writers in general is something generally referred to as style, a quality by no means easy to define. All I can do to differentiate the writers who write with an engaging style from those who don't, is to do it the same way that I differentiate people whom I consider "good company" from those whom I don't like to sit next to at dinner parties.

Not long ago, for instance, I received an issue of *Signature* magazine in the mail and happened to turn to a page that featured an article on Little Cayman, an island in the Caribbean, by a writer named Barbara Currie Maguire, whom I'd never heard of. I read the first paragraph:

Its disciples will tell you quite calmly: There is something *very* different about this island. Lost within that galaxy of coral specks scattered throughout the jade and turquoise Caribbean universe, this tiny isle may also be lost within time.

I immediately closed the magazine. Not because I didn't like what I read, but because I liked it so much, I wanted to save the rest for when I had more time. Barbara Currie Maguire seemed like darn good company.

What is it about Ms. Maguire's paragraph that makes you want to read more—or, at least, made *me* want to read more? It's hard to say. First of all, Ms. Maguire didn't choose to open this piece with the usual boilerplate that sadly characterizes the typical travel article. This told me she was a writer who wasn't content merely to tell me something about this little island, but wanted to tell it in a way I've never heard it told. In other words, she was worried about boring me. But the lead itself—the quiet sureness of it, the lilt and rhythm of that second sentence, nothing cute, nothing forced, nothing overdone, no clichés, just a finely turned sentence with familiar details freshly observed—the lead clinched it.

As it turned out, my suspicion about this writer was correct. She *was* good company. No, her article on Little Cayman will not win a Pulitzer Prize. And most readers, I imagine, will not remember Ms. Maguire's name, even after having read the piece.

But that's not the point. The point is, this little article running no more than five columns in a magazine that goes free to anybody who has a Diner's Club card has a quality that goes beyond standard professionalism. It has a voice of its own. Not an overwhelming nor an intrusive voice, but a voice all the same—a voice that sounds far more refreshing than the voices that characterize most travel articles. Look at this sentence:

> Dense, brooding mangroves enclose the footpath leading to the lake, which suddenly looms, a mirror of pastels and circling herons and frigate birds.

This is not a sentence that flies off anybody's typewriter. You have to visualize the image, get it on paper, and then smooth out its edges. You have to *write* it.

> In the summer rainy season, huge land crabs stampede across the dirt road into the pots of residents.

Granted, all she is telling us is that in the summer rainy season, you can eat big land crabs in Cayman. But, clearly, the writer did not put to typewriter the first thing that popped into her mind. Simply getting the piece *out* of her typewriter was not her prime concern. Her prime concern was giving her reader an experience worth the reader's time. I'd like to talk a little about what writers like Ms. Macguire do to accomplish this aim.

Connecting with Your Reader

By and large, a writer's ability to keep the reader involved will depend mainly on two things: (1) the subject being written about; and (2) the clarity with which it's written. But there's another dynamic at work whenever somebody sits down to read something you've written. It has to do with how much of a *personal* connection you, as a writer, are able to make with your reader, independent of subject matter and independent of clarity.

The "connection" I talk about here is an elusive idea to quantify, but it's basically a matter of the voice you project when you write, and the emotional response (if any) this voice elicits from your reader. In every reader/writer transaction there develops a relationship of sorts, and the dynamics of this relationship are not much different from the dynamics of relationships in general. For the qualities that draw people to one another in relationships are not unlike the qualities that help a writer make a personal connection with his readers. Some writers, by virtue of their style, are warm and easy to be with; you're drawn to them, you feel relaxed and comfortable in their presence. Other writers are easy to take in small doses but too overbearing to stay with for longer periods of time. Some writers are good company because they make you laugh, and some writers are enjoyable to be with simply because you find it easy to identify with them.

All of which is another way of saying that writers, in one way or another, radiate the same qualities that people in general radiate, and that you are drawn to writers or turned off by them for the same reasons you're drawn to or turned off by the qualities of the people with whom you socialize. But there is one quality in particular that unites all good nonfiction writers: they care about you as a reader, and this care is manifest in their style. Good writers don't write for themselves—not primarily, at any rate. They write for their readers. Their object is to *involve* the reader as much as possible in what they're writing. Are there specific techniques that *produce* this involvement? Strictly speaking, no. But there are a number of things these writers do that help create this involvement, and we'll look at them in this chapter.

It Starts with the Lead

I've yet to uncover a "how-to" book on article writing that didn't devote at least one chapter to the so-called *lead*—the first paragraph or two you ask your reader to read. No wonder. One or two paragraphs is about all most readers are going to sample before deciding whether to stay with you or seek diversion elsewhere.

The chief function of the lead, of course, is to let the reader know what you're going to be talking about, but the lead has a less obvious and, in my judgment, equally important function. It lets a reader know whether or not you're going to be "good company."

I cannot overemphasize the importance of your lead as *more* than simply a means of telling your reader what you're writing about. The lead is, in fact, an audition of sorts. Your lead has to do more than convince your reader that you have information that's worth his while to learn. In one way or another, your lead must convince him that you're not taking his interest for granted, that you respect the time he is giving you, that you are going to do everything in your power to reward his trust in you.

Here are a few examples of the leads that seem to me to do just that.

From a *New York Times* piece by Anatole Broyard:

> Arriving at night, my friend from the city pauses before entering the house. "Wow," he says, "look at that moon! It's right out of Magritte."
>
> I look at the moon. It's not out of Magritte. It's out of Connecticut. It's out of this world. It belongs to me, not to the Museum of Modern Art.

This particular essay, as it turns out, deals with the fact that Broyard, who lives in the country, has yet to, as he puts it, "expunge the New Yorker in me." But rather than begin the piece by telling us the nostalgia he sometimes feels for New York, Broyard instead creates a *scene* for us. He introduces us to character, gets us immediately involved in a narrative flow. He's working as hard as he can to *earn* our attention.

Here's one of my favorite openings, from a Paul Pietsch article in *Harper's*.

> Punky was a salamander. Or at least he had the body of a salamander. But his cranium houses the brains of a frog.

You'd never guess at first glance that this is going to be an article about a highly technical subject—holography. Which, I imagine, is why Pietsch decided to start the article in this inviting and highly accessible manner. Indeed, it isn't until six paragraphs later that Pietsch comes out and says, "I will be talking here about the neural hologram." He knows all too well that had he elected to start his article with this statement, he would have immediately lost the majority of his readers.

Now that we've looked at some leads that are actively seeking our involvement, let's look at some that are lacking in reader appeal.

> One of the phenomena of the sexual revolution is that information gleaned from research in the bedroom ends up in the bookstore. Dr. Kinsey set the pace. Masters and Johnson added more factual fuel to the fire, and now Gay Talese is getting into the fray.

There's nothing terribly *wrong* with this lead. But there's nothing compelling about it, either. The first sentence has an interesting idea at its core but the idea comes across rather flat. So do most leads that begin with the phrase "One of the . . . is . . ." And the last two sentences are laced with clichés ("set the pace," "added . . . fuel to the fire," "getting into the fray"). So, here's a lead that suggests the writer doesn't feel obliged to do much more than give me information.

Let's look at another "flat" lead.

> Your car's brake system—partly through manufacturer initiative and partly through government regulation—is

safer, more carefully engineered for emergencies, and probably better overall than the typical brakes were in a car 20 years ago. Brakes are so much better today that drivers tend to ignore them entirely, which is a mistake: nothing's *that* good. Every driver needs to know the brake's basics— how they work, how to monitor them, how to recognize and handle trouble signs.

Let's give this lead a C+. The italicized "that" is the only part of the paragraph that creates any sense of immediacy, and it's a cheap way of creating immediacy at that. How much more impact the same message might have had if the the lead had been written as follows:

Imagine for a moment what it would be like to step on your brakes one day as you're heading for work or the neighborhood supermarket only to discover that your car isn't slowing down. Okay, the chances of this happening to you are remote, but it happens often enough each year in the U.S. that you can never afford to take your brakes for granted. If you drive a car, you need to know something about your brakes—how they work, how to take care of them, and how to tell when your braking system has problems.

The difference here, of course, is that we've involved the reader. Instead of *assuming* he's going to care about his brakes, we've taken it upon ourselves to generate this interest.

The best way to learn to write good leads is to read the major feature magazines and develop a feel for the different *types* of leads you can use. I've chosen several different leads that fall into five different categories. At the very least, you should be able to write each of these types of leads.

The "This Is the Situation" Lead

This is a frequently used and highly versatile type of lead suitable for almost any kind of article, from simple how-to pieces to profiles to first-person reminiscences. Here are some variations on the theme.

From a *Tennis* magazine piece by David Wiltse:

> It is Sunday afternoon and a great experiment in tennis paternalism is about to begin. My wife, Nancy, and I have volunteered to feed and shelter one of the players who will be competing in a big 21-and-under tournament at the nearby Four Seasons Racquet Club in Wilton, Conn. That is, I volunteered after the club posted an appeal in the lobby for player housing and then had to come on like a carpet salesman to convince Nancy what a noble and worthwhile act it would be.

From Jean Vallely's profile of Clint Eastwood, which appeared in *Esquire:*

> The gallery at Pebble Beach couldn't ask for much more than this. Arnold Palmer, Bob Hope and Gerald Ford are all coming into the eighteenth green of the Bing Crosby Pro-Am. They putt out and Hope starts cracking jokes, Ford starts working the crowd, and Palmer grins, giving autographs. Susan Ford, the former President's peppy daughter, is there, clicking away with her Nikon. Happy faces, television cameras, a smooth green and the Pacific Ocean—it's like a Coca-Cola commercial, albeit with slightly overage actors. Then a tall man comes walking alone up the fairway. He looks menacing.

The "I Want You to Focus on a Specific Detail" Lead

The idea here is to take something specific—somebody's car or house or face or painting—and build your opening around it. If done well, this lead works effectively because it gets your reader to narrow his focus at the outset. Here's a good illustration of the technique from Aaron Latham's *Esquire* piece on Clark Clifford:

> Clark Clifford's face looks as if it belonged on a hundred-dollar bill. It has that patrician expression which the Founding Fathers usually assumed when they posed for their legal tender portraits. The perfect nose and the wavy hair add a classical touch, so the face would not look out of place stamped on a Roman coin, either. At any rate, when you look at Clark Clifford, you think of money: old money, new money, but mainly lots of money.

The "Imagine What It Would Be Like If" Lead

In this kind of lead, you draw your reader in by placing him in a hypothetical situation that is keyed to his interests—or, better, survival. Here's an example from a piece I did years ago for *Signature*.

> I would like you to imagine for a moment that you are a highly placed executive for a large corporation and that at this very moment you are sitting in the reception lounge of a local television station. Across from you sits a keyed-up young woman who is known throughout the city for being the most militant spokesperson for women's rights and who has publically accused your corporation of being "criminally anti-female in its hiring practices." Next to her sits a ruggedly earnest-looking fellow in a lumberjack and hiking boots who represents a local environmental group. He holds in his lap a knapsack that contains, he has just told you, photographs of animals that have died as the result of a pollutant supposedly created as a by-product of your company's manufacturing process. Within five minutes, the three of you are going to be the guests of a local talk show personality—a man whom the head of your company's public relations department has described as a "glib snake who loves to bait big business."

The "Let Me Tell You Who I Am and Why I'm Writing This" Lead

This type of lead works well in first-person pieces in which you as the narrator are going to share equal billing with the subject. Here's novelist J. Bryan III, leading off a *Travel & Leisure* piece on martinis:

> Just to establish my credentials, let me testify that I have drunk martinis all around the world, except in the longitudes between Delhi and Perth. I have drunk them based on bathtub gin and 70-proof Australian gin and the finest English gin. I have drunk them made half-and-half with sweet Italian vermouth (that one I can still taste!)—for want of any vermouth at all—with dry sherry, and with beer whipped until it was flat (not so bad as it may sound). I have drunk them lukewarm, out of jelly glasses, paper cups and pewter mugs.

The "General (and, One Hopes, Sage) Observation" Lead

In this type of a lead, you begin by making a general observation and then tie it somehow to your subject. This is a risky lead because even good writers have a tendency to sound pontifical when presented with a soap box. So if you're using this type of lead—and in some situations, it works—don't go overboard. Some examples worth emulating.

From Peter Andrews's *Signature* piece on Muzak:

> Like bubble gum and McDonald's hamburgers, Muzak is one of those unique American creations the whole world seems to have taken to its heart in spite of the fact that many people who are supposed to know about such things keep saying they're bad for us. Certainly any member of the

artistic elite who wants to go "cluck cluck" over the state of culture in America has only to mention the phrase "music by Muzak" to pick up a quick laugh from his audience.

From one of my pieces in *Playbill:*

It is sometimes more difficult—and always less rewarding—to maintain standards than to establish them. The New York City Ballet is probably the best dressed ballet company in the world, and this, of course, is due largely to designer and couturière Madame Karinska, whose costumes characteristically reveal an almost Fabergé-like devotion to detail. But whereas Madame Karinska's responsibility leaves off the day her costumes arrive at the New York State Theater, the responsibility of Madame Sophie Pourmel and Leslie "Ducky" Copeland is just beginning. They are the respective women's and men's wardrobe supervisors for the New York City Ballet, and it's up to them and their respective assistants, Corniele DeBrauw and Arthur Craig, to make sure that Madame Karinska's costumes enjoy a long and distinguished life. It is anything but a simple matter.

The "Flood Your Reader with Details" Lead

In this type of lead, you give your readers quick takes of information that generate the flavor and the substance of the material you're about to cover. Janet Coleman uses this kind of lead to good advantage in an article called "Hey, That Sounds Like What's-His-Name" published in *New York* magazine:

"Talent" in the advertising world means anyone who is seen or heard on a television or radio commercial. That includes actors, announcers, people with nice feet, Rocky Graziano, gas station attendants, football stars, animals. International Famous Agency represents a little dog who does a back-flip and an actor who can imitate termites. I know an actress who makes a living off the residuals of her two pet chimpanzees. A casting bulletin that circulated around the advertising agencies announced, "Available: Timothy Leary, of Harvard and LSD." One New York Talent agency has a chart in the lobby listing all its clients under the headings Teeth, Legs, Hands, Lips, Voice, Dentures. My own husband, David Dozer, recently acquired something of a reputation as a professional hand model. He played a pair of hands that washed themselves with Zest soap in the back of a crowded elevator.

You'll notice that Ms. Coleman doesn't worry too much in this paragraph about transitions, and it's true there are more than a few abrupt focus shifts in this paragraph. But you can get away with this "shotgun" approach for a paragraph or two, providing your details are interesting enough. Indeed, when you're piling on detail after detail, transitions are too cumbersome a device to use easily and effectively. Transitions are also noticeable by their absence in the following lead, which comes from a piece on tennis-playing senators I once wrote for *U.S. Air* magazine.

Charles Percy, the Republican senator from Illinois, and chairman of the Senate Foreign Relations Committee, was talking tough: This time out, he warned (in contrast, you understand, to the electoral landslide last November), the Republicans weren't going to play Mr. Nice Guy. Lloyd Bentsen, the tall, courtly Democratic senator from Texas, was amused. He hadn't been this scared, he allowed, since he got word from Chicken Little that the sky was falling. J. Bennett Johnston, the slim soft-spoken Democratic senator from Louisiana, chided the Republicans for being "arrogant," adding he wasn't surprised at all since they were, after all, Republicans. And Lowell Weicker, the not so slim and not so quiet Connecticut Republican (whom you may remember from the Watergate hearings) said that the Democrats were being "self-righteous," but added he wasn't surprised since when did anybody meet a Democratic politician who *wasn't* self-righteous. And on and on.

Creating More Immediacy in Your Writing

Immediacy, as I mentioned in Chapter 1, is hard to define, but I like to think of it as the quality which secures the writer's "connection" with his reader—that is, the ability to make the reader *experience* more directly what you're writing. Immediacy is related, in part, to your choice of words—the more specific and concrete your language, the easier you make it for the reader to get involved. But there are other techniques as well which help to produce the immediacy that distinguishes the accomplished writer from the mediocre.

Setting a Scene

Accomplished nonfiction writers will frequently use a scene as a means of introducing a person they're going to be talking about or else to pave the way for expository information. Scene-setting is an effective device because it helps the reader identify more with the material by giving him a sense of place. Let's look at some examples.

From an Adam Smith column in *Esquire:*

> Recently I met a very famous economist at a club dinner. The gentlemen were properly attired in their dinner jackets, chuckling urbanely to one another, and in their midst was a smallish, grey-haired, very lively man telling stories in a Mel Brooks–Carl Reiner Russian accent—an accent that was real, however, and that only added to his charm. The story teller was Wassily Leontief, and he is famous for at least two reasons.

Strictly speaking, Smith didn't really *need* the middle sentence to introduce us to Leontief, but the details in the beginning of that second sentence help us to settle into the scene and serve as staging devices for the arrival of the main character.

Here's John Van Doorn, from a *New York* magazine article called "An Intimidating New Class: The Physical Elite." Notice how Van Doorn's use of *sounds* gives added immediacy to the passage.

> That evening a great number of them were gathered in the Palace Hotel, where a backgammon tournament was in progress. Old acquaintances showed their teeth at each other, arranged into smiles. Dice clacked in cups, pieces clicked around boards. It sounded like beetles mating. Beside the telephone, a telex stuttered out the prices in Zurich, Frankfurt, Tokyo, and New York.

If there is a single key to the scene-setting technique, it lies in your ability to compress as many details as possible in your two or three scene-setting sentences. Remember, your objective is mainly to give your reader a sense of *being* there.

Here's Sandy Treadwell exemplifying the technique in a piece he wrote for *Sports Illustrated* on umpire Eric Gregg:

> The Atlanta Braves sat in their dugout last Friday evening and quietly observed the Opening Day ceremonies. A choir sang, a former hostage in Iran threw out the first ball, fireworks exploded and Umpire Eric Gregg, 106 pounds lighter than he was at the end of the season, walked onto the field.

Two sentences, five details. What they do is to get us *into* a scene. Interestingly enough, you rarely need more than a sentence or two, or four or five precise details, to make your reader feel closer to your material, so even when your space is limited, you can still work these details in.

To help engrave this principle in your mind, look at the following student example, and then at the revision, to see what a difference a simple reader-involvement phrase can make.

> Recently I had a wrestling match with a large rock which occupied some space I had a need for. The rock was odd in shape and when I tried to get a grip on it, it was as ungrippable as certain memories which occupy space in my mind— space which I also have a need for. Eventually, I dislodged this rock but it's not easy with memories. They stick tenaciously in the soil of the mind.

In the following revision, I'll italicize the phrases that help make the reader feel a part of the scene.

> Recently I had a wrestling match with a large rock which occupied some space *in my front yard* that I had a need for. It was a rather large rock, *twice the size of a football,* but size wasn't the problem. The rock had an odd shape. It was ungrippable—as ungrippable as certain memories which occupy space in my mind that I also have a need for. Eventually, I was able to dislodge this rock, *by shoving it this way and that,* but it's not easy to dislodge memories: memories stick much more tenaciously in the soil of the mind.

Letting Down Your Hair

English is rich in idioms, yet surprisingly few writers use them effectively. True, the line between an idiom and a cliché isn't always clearly defined, but a judiciously placed idiom (and even a cliché, if it's used properly) can give your writing more zip, more flavor, more readability. Here are several brief passages that work all the better because of the idiomatic language.

From Frank Deford's *Sports Illustrated* profile of Chris Evert:

During these years, there were some ballyhooed romances with the likes of Burt Reynolds and a President's son, Jack Ford, as Chris' schoolgirl dreams of finding a Shining Knight behind the picket fence next door were fading. She was, in effect, pricing herself out of that neighborhood.

It isn't only the idioms themselves—"Shining Knight," "pricing herself out of the neighborhood"—that spice this presentation, but also the way Deford *uses* them. "Shining Knight behind the picket fence next door" suggests that Chris, by looking for the ideal lovemate in her own backyard, was setting impossible standards for herself. And "pricing herself out of the neighborhood" uses a phrase you would normally associate with real estate to express the idea of Chris looking beyond the "boy next door." Using idioms in so freewheeling a manner is a tricky technique to master, but it will serve you well if you can do it comfortably.

From Tom Wolfe, who may be the most idiomatic of today's nonfiction writers, a passage from *The Right Stuff*:

All these people with their smiles of sympathy didn't ask for much. A few words here and there would do fine. *Do good work.* Nevertheless, that didn't make these public appearances any better for Cooper. He was in the same boat with Gus and Deke, who was also no Franklin D. Roosevelt when it came to public appearances. Everybody latched on to you during these trips, congressmen and businessmen and directors and presidents of this and that. Every hotshot in town wanted to be next to the *astronaut.* . . .

The only side of the whole deal that appeared to shake Cooper's confidence was the p.r. side of it, the publicity routine, the trips here and there, where various local worthies put you at the head table and whacked you on the back and asked you to get up and "just say a few words."

Actually, it's tough to find *any* paragraph in Wolfe's book that doesn't contain at least one phrase that your fifth-grade English teacher would have criticized for being too colloquial. Indeed, writing teachers are forever cautioning their students not to emulate writers like Wolfe and Hunter Thompson and others who use lots of colloquialisms. Maybe these teachers are right—Wolfe's is a distinctive voice and you can sound very silly trying to emulate him. Yet, the problem I run into with most of the students in my writing classes isn't that they are *too* colloquial but rather that they aren't colloquial enough. Their writing tends to be overly formal. One of my assignments each semester directs my students to write a short paragraph as if they were Tom Wolfe, and I get some surprisingly nice writing. It's possible that you, too, could benefit from this kind of exercise, in which you consciously emulate the style of a writer like Wolfe or Thompson. The idea, remember, isn't to write exactly like either of them, but to nourish your style with those idiomatic elements it may now lack.

Using "You"

Most of us were cautioned early in our schooling that there is no room in "good" writing for the second-person pronoun. Odd, then, that good writers rely on the second-person construction in a variety of situations. Apart from the obvious—that "you" speaks directly to the reader and gets him involved—I'm not sure why it's so effective when used in the right place. But effective it is. Here are some examples of "you" in action.

From Lewis Thomas's essay "Germs" which appears in *Lives of a Cell*.

> Watching television, you'd think we lived at bay, in total jeopardy, surrounded on all sides by human-seeking germs,

shielded against infection and death only by a chemical technology that enables us to keep killing them off.

The "you" in this case sets the easy conversational tone of the essay—important since Thomas writes about scientific topics for a largely *non*-scientific audience.

From Peter Andrews's *Signature* piece on Muzak:

> If you are one of the incorrigible few who doesn't like Muzak, just trying getting away from it, especially in a large building. If you don't hear it in the typing pool or over the telephone or in the lobby, Muzak will get you in the elevator or rest room.

From Paul Theroux, in *The Great Railway Bazaar:*

> The hotel is empty; the other guests have risked a punishing journey to Swat in hopes of being received by His Highness the Wali. You sleep soundly under a tent of mosquito net and are awakened by the fluting of birds for an English breakfast that begins with porridge and ends with a kidney.

Here "you" is a substitute for "I," which some purists might find a little forced. I like—and use—the substitution often because it gives first-person narrative and descriptive writing a greater sense of immediacy. Here's how I used the construction in a description of the Monte Carlo Country Club I did for *Town & Country*.

> . . . The surface is red clay—a surface you rarely see in the U.S. anymore because it requires almost as much maintenance as grass—and the overall area is so large, with so much room between the courts, a more frugal builder could have easily squeezed in another court. You do not see a fence: it is there forming the standard perimeter, but it is buried within the verdant embrace of a tall hedge.

The Parenthetical Aside

The parenthetical aside is a simple technique in which you interrupt a sentence with a piece of related but not directly connected information set off from the rest of the sentence with either parenthesis or a dash. What this technique seems to do is reinforce *your* presence in the reader's mind. It's also a useful technique to relieve the monotony of a passage filled with mainly expository details. An example from Nora Ephron's essay "Consciousness Raising":

> At each meeting we would choose a topic—mothers, success, sex, femininity, and orgasms were a few we took on at the start—and it was really like being part of a novel unfolding, as every week the character of each woman became clearer and more detailed.

And one from *Sports Illustrated* writer Doug Looney:

> It is a terrible blow to a person (heck, let's use me as an example) who does so many things brilliantly to find out that putting up a basketball hoop is not one of them.

One word of caution: as useful as this technique is, particularly in humanizing your presentation, don't go overboard with it. Three or four times in an average-length piece (about 2,500 words) is enough. More than this, and the technique becomes too obvious and mannered.

Getting into
Print

IT'S one thing to learn how to write well enough to publish pieces in magazines and newspapers and something else again actually to break into print. To be sure, you're not going to make much headway in the commercial writing field unless you are reasonably skilled at the craft, but there is a good deal more to getting editors to buy and publish your material than being a skilled craftsman. And if you're looking to make a decent living as a writer, these other nonwriting considerations assume even more importance. I can introduce you to people who write remarkably well and yet have never published *anything,* and I can introduce you to people with only mediocre writing skills who are earning a comfortable living. The difference: the people who are making a living at writing understand the *business* aspect of the craft. And more than understand it, they're willing to gear what they do to the realities of the marketplace.

I have been a full-time freelance writer since the mid-1960s and, except for the course I have been teaching at Fairfield University for the past four years, I have earned my living entirely as a writer. I have written, co-written, or ghost-written twenty books, and more articles than I can count, and I have also written ad copy, brochures, speeches, and film strips. For a brief period during the late 1960s I even wrote the little squibs you often see on menus. A lot of this writing I did not necessarily *want* to do. I did it because I needed the money.

It's safe to say, I think, that most people who earn their living as writers produce the majority of the things they write for the same reason: it pays the bills. Needless to say, those of us who write full-time derive personal satisfaction from what we do, and enjoy the fact that as freelance writers we're spared the nine-to-five grind that most people take for granted. But the number of writers who are in a position to write only what they feel inspired to write is very small indeed. Even a writer as celebrated as Norman Mailer is denied this luxury.

I bring up the money aspect of writing because no other factor I can think of will have a more direct bearing on how you plan and pursue your writing career. If you are financially secure enough to write and publish purely for the fun of it, with money merely a secondary consideration (if so, I'll change places with you today), you can handle the career aspects of writing far differently from somebody who is writing to pay the rent and food bills. You can be more selective about the markets you pursue. You can take more time on the articles you're assigned. You may not write as *much* as other writers, but you'll probably enjoy it more.

On the other hand, if money *is* a consideration, you have to think of yourself less as a creative artist and more as a businessman who has a product to sell and markets to satisfy. This isn't to say that you shouldn't take what you write seriously; nor is it to say that you have to be entirely "commercial" in your career strategy. But if you don't take a reasonably businesslike and professional attitude to your writing, your career will never get off the ground, or, if it does, you'll have a bumpy ride indeed. Perhaps some of what I have to say in this chapter will make things a little easier for you.

Breaking into a Magazine

Before I sold my first piece to *Playbill* magazine in the mid-1960s, I had written the editor Joan Rubin four letters with article suggestions over a period of eighteen months. The first three letters drew polite rejections. The fourth expressed an interest in one of several ideas I presented. The idea had to do with Broadway actors and actresses who were earning extra money by doing television and radio commercials. "I like the idea," Joan Rubin said when we spoke by phone. "Would you mind doing it on 'spec.'?"

What Ms. Rubin was asking me to do here, of course, was to write the article on "speculation"—with no guarantee that she would publish it. In other words, she had no abiding faith in my ability to write it. Then again, she had no *reason* to have any faith since I'd never written for her and could only show, by way of past work, some newspaper articles I'd done in the army and a few articles on restaurants I'd done for a hotel magazine I was working on at the time.

"I'll tell you what," I said, looking to make a deal and salvage my ego at the same time. "If the *only* thing you're concerned about is whether or not I can write this piece, I'm happy to do it. But I have to know you really like the idea."

"I definitely like the idea," she said.

"Then I'll write it," I said.

And I did. It was called "Moonlighting on Madison Avenue," and Joan liked it. I was paid, I think, three hundred dollars. More important, on the day Joan called to tell me she liked the piece, she asked me if I would like to do an article for the opera *Playbill*. *Asked* me. I didn't have to write four letters, or an outline. I didn't even have to do the piece on speculation. I was getting an assignment I never sought. And whereas my first assignment for *Playbill* had taken me more than eighteen months to get, the second took all of ten seconds.

For better or for worse, the writing business is like this. Editors are gun-shy if you haven't yet proven yourself, but once you show them that you can do the job and that you're easy to get along with, the whole business of getting assignments becomes infinitely easier and less time-consuming. The problem, of course, is getting that first shot.

My advice on getting a magazine or a newspaper to give you at least a chance to show what you can do is that you put yourself in the shoes of the person in charge of assignments. Why should this person assign *you* a particular article? What do you have to offer that other writers the editor knows (and can depend on) can't handle as well as you?

The answer, simply, is that you have to come up with some compelling idea. And more than a compelling idea— an idea that you are uniquely qualified to write. For instance, when I pitched Joan Rubin on my actors-on-Madison-Avenue idea, I mentioned some actors I knew who were appearing in commercials. I mentioned an agent I knew who was willing to give me a lot of anecdotes. I mentioned an advertising executive who had promised to let me view the making of a commercial. In short, I did my best to convince Joan that she was better off with *me* handling this idea than she was with a writer she already knew.

You have to do the same thing. A profile on, say, Paul Newman is a saleable idea, but why should an editor hire *you* to write it when he knows two dozen or so writers who can—and would love to—write the same profile? You may have some interesting ideas on the economy, but if you're not an economist, the editor is going to figure that his readers won't be interested, and you won't be assigned an article that gives *your* views on the economy.

So what you have to look for, at least until you've established some sort of track record, are ideas that give the editor a reason for choosing you for the job. The fact that you *thought up* the idea isn't enough: you have to ask yourself, what reason am I giving this editor to assign *me*?

Choose the magazine you're looking to sell your first piece to with care. As a general rule, the more prestigious and more successful the magazine, the tougher it is for a writer without credentials to break in. If I were a writer who hadn't yet published anything, I would first approach local newspapers or regional magazines. They don't pay much, but at least the clipping gives you something to send to an editor of another magazine. Once I had a few credits in these local magazines, I would try to sell to some of the airline magazines. And not until after I'd gained a foothold in this market would I make a bid to sell to the big national magazines like *Reader's Digest, Playboy, Ladies' Home Journal, Cosmopolitan,* etc.

That's *my* approach. This isn't to say that if you have a compelling enough idea, you can't go directly to a national magazine, sell it, and spare yourself the slow climb to this level. What happened in my career was this: after selling four or five pieces to *Playbill,* I wrote a piece for *New York* magazine on how to park your car in Manhattan, basing my pitch on the fact that as somebody who drove into the city everyday I'd become something of an expert. ("How-to" pieces, incidentally, are the easiest pieces for unpublished writers to sell, largely because a lot of established writers don't like to write them.) *New York* liked the parking piece and over the next several months assigned me a number of other "how-to" pieces, which I did happily. My *New York* pieces eventually opened doors to other magazines like *Town & Country, Signature, Travel & Leisure,* and *Sport,* among others. What's more, as editors I've worked with at various magazines have changed jobs, they have often pro-

vided me entry to their *new* magazine. Recently, for instance, an editor I worked with years ago at *Sport* became
an editor at *Reader's Digest,* and the relationship looks as
if it is going to produce my first *Reader's Digest* assignment.

Then again, it has taken me nearly twenty years to get
established—to reach a point where I can call an editor
directly to find out if he or she is interested in an idea and
if it's worth putting the idea down on paper, twenty years
to reach a point where an editor will call *me* with an idea.
How have I done it? There is no one answer, but here are
some suggestions that have served me well as a freelancer
and could work for you.

1. Develop a Specialty

It can be almost anything—business, sports, finance, sci-
ence, gardening, food and drink, antiques, etc.—and it
doesn't have to be the *only* thing you write about. There are
two good reasons for developing a specialty. For one thing,
the more you know about a particular field, the easier it is
going to be for you to research and write about subjects
within the specialty. It means that you can write in three
days an article that might take somebody else two weeks.
Secondly, editors of general-interest magazines tend to
seek out writers whom they identify with a particular field
or subject. In the early 1970s, for instance, I worked on two
different guides to tennis resorts in the United States and
suddenly found myself one of the country's leading author-
ities on the subject. Since then, I've published at least a
dozen articles in various magazines about how to plan and
where to go on a tennis vacation, each article with its own
slant but each making use of the same basic research. I
would hope that by the time I wind up my writing career, I
will have made a mark in a specialty other than tennis

vacations, but in the meantime writing these articles has helped to pay the rent.

2. Develop a "Marketing" Routine

Just as it's a good idea to develop a set routine for doing your writing, it also makes good sense to set up some routine for dealing with the career aspects of writing. Try to spend at least three or four hours a week looking over magazines and reading local newspapers and scientific journals that might produce ideas. Set goals for yourself. Force yourself to write (provided you're not inundated with assignments) at least three or four query letters a week and don't allow yourself to be discouraged by the rejection slips. Keep knocking on the door.

3. Separate Your Ego from Your Work

The surest way to drive yourself nuts as a writer is to get your ego too wrapped up in your work. If you're overly sensitive to what other people have to say about your writing, you will spare yourself a good deal of misery by choosing some other line of work. I like most of the editors I know, but, as a group, I wouldn't classify book editors and magazine editors as paragons of tact. Editors have a job to do: to assign pieces and to see to it that the pieces meet their criteria for publication. Looking out for your feelings isn't part of the job.

4. Make Things Easy for Your Editors

Most editors on magazines today are overworked and the more you can do to make their lives less hassled, the easier it's going to be for you to sell them pieces. If you promise to deliver a manuscript on a particular date, keep your promise, and if you see you're running behind, have the courtesy to let the editor know well ahead of time so he can make his plans accordingly. If an editor asks for revisions, don't take it personally: editors know their readers better than you do.

5. *Don't Squabble about Money*

Don't make unreasonable money demands of the editors you work with, not unless you're independently wealthy or have more assignments than you can handle. Most magazines have a fairly standard fee schedule: so many dollars for one type of article; a little more or less for another type of article. You have a right to know, of course, before you start an article how much money the magazine intends to pay you, how much they're willing to give you in expense money, and if they have a so-called "kill" fee—that is, money they will pay you in the event they don't publish your article. I suppose if you complain enough, you can get most editors to pay you an additional fifty or a hundred dollars for a piece, but my suspicion is they won't go out of their way to assign you additional pieces.

How to Write a Query Letter

A query letter, of course, is a letter to an editor of a magazine in which you present an idea and try to convince the editor that you're the person to write it. There is no great mystery to writing a good query letter. It's simply a matter of presenting an idea that at least has a shot at drawing the editor's interest, and writing the letter well enough so that the editor isn't afraid to give you the assignment.

I follow a simple system in the query letters I submit, as

the letter on pages 182–83 indicates. I divide the letter into four sections.

1. *Making the connection.* In the first paragraph, I try to make some personal connection with the specific editor. I'll mention the name of a person who suggested that I write the editor. I'll mention an article I've read in the editor's magazine that made me think he'd be interested in my idea. In this paragraph I try to give the editor a reason for reading the rest of the letter, and I generally present a very broad idea of what I want to do.

2. *Getting the editor interested.* In the second section of the letter, which can be a paragraph or two, I try to get the editor interested in the subject and do my best to show how interested the readers of the magazine will be in the article I'm suggesting. I do this by providing specific information and not merely by asserting that readers will like what I'm suggesting.

3. *Getting more specific.* In the third section, I give the editor a brief but reasonably detailed idea of how I intend to write the article: the kind of information that I'll include, the slant I'll take, the people I intend to interview, etc.

4. *Closing.* In the last section of the letter, I let the editor know my willingness to talk about the subject in more depth and offer to supply any additional information the editor might want. I also thank the editor ahead of time for the consideration he may give my article idea.

General Guidelines for Query Letters

1. Be brief.

2. Make sure that the idea you suggest is (1) appropriate for the magazine you're writing to; and (2) has not been covered by that magazine recently.

3. If you can make some personal connection early in the letter ("So-and-so suggested I write you . . ."), do so.

4. Be upbeat and positive but don't oversell. Avoid overstatement, and don't hit the editor over the head with how much he needs the article you're selecting. Let the editor decide.

5. Be as specific as you can in outlining the general content of your article.

6. Try to write naturally. Avoid formal phrases like "It has come to my attention . . ."

7. If the editor doesn't know you or your work, send along a representative piece or two. It should be a published piece—not a term paper or manuscript.

8. Avoid cute expressions and don't beat around the bush. Letters that try to titillate without getting substantial usually end up in the trash basket.

Sample Query Letter

Christine Donaldson
Articles Editor
Home Living Magazine
430 Madison Ave.
New York, N.Y. 10017

Dear Ms. Donaldson:

Get the editor's attention

I'm writing you at the suggestion of Jacqueline Onassis, who felt that a project I'm currently involved with might be of some interest to you.

[or]

Over the past several months, I've noticed that Home Living has been running a number of articles on businesses you can start on your own at home. I am currently operating one that might well be of interest to your readers.

Get to the point

Essentially what I have been doing is training ants to do basic clean-up work around the house. I have been involved in this business for six months and I now have ten different work crews I hire out on a daily basis to people in my neighborhood. Because the ants do not eat much and are not unionized, I have been able to average $100 a week.

Tell what you intend to do in the article. Be specific

The article I envision would tell your readers just about everything they need to set up their own ant housecleaning business: how to select the right ants, how to train them, how to drum up business, and how to set up a workable bookkeeping system.

Provide an additional "push"...

For your further information, I have enclosed a copy of an article I wrote recently for a local newspaper on ant recruitment. It should give you an idea of the material and of how I write. If you want additional information, please let me know.

I look forward to hearing from you.

Sincerely,

Abby Smith

FURTHER READING

Bates, Jefferson D. *Writing With Precision*. 2nd ed. Washington, D.C.: Acropolis, 1978.

Bernstein, Theodore M. *The Careful Writer: A Modern Guide to English Usage*. New York: Atheneum, 1980 (1965).

Berry, Thomas Elliott. *The Craft of Writing*. New York: McGraw Hill, 1974.

Driskill, L. P., and Simpson, Margaret. *Decisive Writing: An Improvement Program*. New York: Oxford University Press, 1978.

Elbow, Peter. *Writing with Power*. New York: Oxford University Press, 1981.

Graves, Robert, and Hodge, Alan. *The Reader Over Your Shoulder*. 2nd ed. New York: Vintage, 1979.

Mack, Karin, and Skjei, Eric. *Overcoming Writing Blocks*. Los Angeles: J. P. Tarcher, 1979.

Montgomery, Michael, and Stratton, John. *The Writer's Hotline Handbook: A Guide to Good Usage and Effective Writing*. New York: New American Library, 1981.

Payne, Lucile Vaughan. *The Lively Art of Writing*. New York: New American Library, 1965.

Provost, Gary. *Make Every Word Count*. Cincinnati: Writer's Digest Books, 1980.

Strunk, William Jr., and White, E. B. *The Elements of Style*. 3rd ed. New York: Macmillan, 1979.

Zinsser, William. *On Writing Well: An Informal Guide to Writing Nonfiction*. 2nd ed. New York: Harper & Row, 1980.